Environment, development, agriculture

Environment, development, agriculture
Integrated policy through human ecology

Bernhard Glaeser
Social Science Research Center Berlin (WZB)

M.E. Sharpe
Armonk, New York
London, England

First published in 1995 by UCL Press

UCL Press Limited
University College London
Gower Street
London WC1E 6BT

The name of University College London (UCL) is a registered trade mark used by UCL Press with the consent of the owner.

Library of Congress Cataloging-in-Publication Data

Glaeser, Bernhard.
Environment, development, agriculture: integrated policy through human ecology/
Bernhard Glaeser.
p. cm.
Includes bibliographical references and index.
ISBN 1-56324-692-9 (hardcover). — ISBN 1-56324-693-7 (pbk.)
1. Sustainable development.
2. Sustainable agriculture.
3. Human ecology.
4. Environmental ethics.
I. Title.
HC79. E5G57 1995
338.1—dc20
95-23920
CIP

(c)   10   9   8   7   6   5   4   3   2   1
(p)   10   9   8   7   6   5   4   3   2   1

Typeset in Zapf Elliptical.
Printed and bound by
Biddles Ltd, Guildford and King's Lynn, England.

Contents

Preface

The physical human environment, in a broader sense "nature", has been of basic importance for the economic development of human societies. This has been true throughout the history of humankind, yet it has been only recently that economic development began to threaten its own basis, that is the very existence of nature of which humans are a part. Does humankind have a right, perhaps a human right, over nature? This is one of the fundamental issues of environmental ethics, which is reflected in some of the environmental principles upon which members of the United Nations Organization (UNO) have agreed.

Principle 1 of the Stockholm Declaration on the Human Environment (UNCHE 1973: 19) states:

> Man has the fundamental right to freedom, equality and adequate conditions of life, in an environment of a quality that permits a life of dignity and wellbeing, and he bears a solemn responsibility to protect and improve the environment for present and future generations . . .

These words state not only a fundamental human right concerning the environment but, more importantly, they imply a fundamental responsibility of human beings and a "right of nature" to be protected from man. Principle 4 of the Declaration supports this interpretation of Principle 1:

> Man has a special responsibility to safeguard and wisely manage the heritage of wildlife and its habitat . . . Nature conservation . . . must therefore receive importance in planning for economic development. (UNCHE 1973: 19)

Ecology and (economic) development have been combined to form the concept of "ecodevelopment", which means the purpose of development is not solely to enhance economic growth. Development must be sustainable: it should preserve and improve the environmental basis for economic development. This is obviously what the United Nations Conference on the

Human Environment (UNCHE) and the Stockholm Declaration of 1972 intended: development policy in accordance with nature and environment.

The 1992 United Nations Conference on Environment and Development (UNCED) acknowledged the fact that humanity's relationship to nature and the use of resources and ecological services, has almost never been considered important. The scientific discipline of human ecology provides a framework for thought and research along these lines, not only from a political perspective, but also from the point of view of theory and ethics.

The present volume focuses on aspects of philosophy and social science in human ecology and includes case examples concerning political implementation. Part One deals with aspects of theory, including a comprehensive introduction to the field as well as an overview of typical conceptual modelling in human ecology. Part Two moves from theoretical, historical and methodological questions to those of human behaviour and action. The relationship between environmental ethics and environmental policy is explored in terms of aspects of justification and implementation in human interactions with nature and the environment in an ecologically sustaining way. Two examples illustrate what is meant by ecologically sustainable development in the third part: a review of environmental policy in the People's Republic of China since 1949, and a regional case study including a policy recommendation from India. Whereas the former is historically orientated towards actual intentions and achievements, the latter is outlook-orientated in that it examines future opportunities for environmental planning involving local people and their specific cultural settings. Prospects for the future are taken up on a more general basis in the final part of the book. The chapter on agrarian culture criticizes present North–South relations, including colonial history and development, and it makes a point in favour of ecological and cultural variety in agriculture. In the final chapter, the relation between nature and culture is reconsidered theoretically, and it is argued that, strictly speaking, there is no such thing as nature in crisis. Rather, overexploitation of the environment – and thus the destruction of natural living conditions – reflects a state of cultural crisis in "ill" human societies.

By and large, my approach to the above issues, in particular the question of the relationship between ethics and environmental policy, has its roots in the German intellectual–philosophical and social science tradition. With the exception of Immanuel Kant I have translated quotations from German authors myself. Thus there are two page references for each Kant quotation, the first referring to the German original, the second to the translation.

The analysis of conceptual and applied models in human ecology in Chapters 1 and 2 is largely based on a combined study by Kevin D. Phillips-Howard and myself.[1] This applies specifically to §1.3 and §2.2.

I gratefully acknowledge extremely helpful comments from Ulrich Loening[2], Kevin Phillips-Howard[3] and Bill Puka[4] at the manuscript stage, the translation of parts of this book by Peter Germain (Ch. 8) and Jerry Hodges (Chs 1, 3, 4 and 7) and the invaluable assistance of my editor, Niamh Warde, in identifying and eliminating inconsistencies and redundancies, and in ironing out the other rough spots in this book. Needless to say, any remaining errors are my own.

Berlin, September 1994
Bernhard Glaeser

1. K. D. Phillips-Howard & B. Glaeser, "Comparative investigation of conceptual models in human ecology", Science and Public Policy, 10–20, 1983 (February).
2. Centre of Human Ecology, University of Edinburgh, UK.
3. Department of Geography, University of Transkei, Umtata, Southern Africa.
4. Department of Philosophy, Rensselaer Polytechnic Institute, Troy, USA.

Acknowledgements

Much of this book draws on previously published articles, some of which were originally written in German. All have been amended and updated.

Chapter 1

Glaeser, B. 1988. A holistic human ecology approach to sustainable agricultural development. *Futures* **20**(6), 671–8.
Glaeser, B. 1989. Entwurf einer Humanökologie. In *Humanökologie: Grundlagen präventiver Umweltpolitik*, B. Glaeser (ed.), 27–45. Opladen, Germany: Westdeutscher.

Chapters 1 and 2

Phillips-Howard, K. D. & B. Glaeser 1983. Comparative investigation of conceptual models in human ecology. *Science and Public Policy* (February), 10–20.

Chapter 3

Glaeser, B. 1989. Möglichkeiten und Grenzen einer Umweltethik. In *Humanökologie: Grundlagen präventiver Umweltpolitik*, B. Glaeser (ed.), 113–18. Opladen, Germany: Westdeutscher.

Chapter 4

Glaeser, B. 1989. Umweltpolitik – Neuansatz in der Spannung zwischen Theorie und Praxis. In *Humanökologie: Grundlagen präventiver Umweltpolitik*, B. Glaeser (ed.), 11–24. Opladen, Germany: Westdeutscher.

Chapter 5

Glaeser, B. 1990. The environmental impact of economic development: problems and policies. In *The geography of contemporary China: the impact of*

Deng Xiaoping's decade, T. Cannon & A. Jenkins (eds), 249–65. London: Routledge.

Chapter 6

Glaeser, B. 1989. An eco-development approach for the Andaman and Nicobar Islands. In *Economic development alternatives: Andaman and Nicobar Islands*, B. R. Virmani and K. J. Voll (eds), 120–31. New Delhi: Vision

Chapter 7

Glaeser, B. 1989. Human ecology in Germany: research focus "agrarian culture". In *Human ecology – coming of age: an international overview*, S. Suzuki, R. J. Borden, L. Hens (eds), 143–64. Brussels: VUB-Press.

Chapter 8

Glaeser, B. 1992. Natur in der Krise? Ein kulturelles Mißverständnis. In *Humanökologie und Kulturökologie*, B. Glaeser & P. Teherani-Krönner (eds), 49–70. Opladen, Germany: Westdeutscher.

PART ONE
A theoretical paradigm

CHAPTER 1
An outline of human ecology

This chapter sets out to provide an introduction to human ecology. The intention is to acquaint the reader with the substance and problems of this still young science. In so doing, attention is given to a portrayal of so-called established knowledge, but also to the author's own point of view. The following questions will be dealt with in detail.

What is human ecology? §1.1, "The concept and its delimitation", is concerned with the starting point of human ecology in "environmental science", on the one hand, and ecology, to which it owes its concept, on the other. In addition, Chapter 1 shows how human ecology can be incorporated into various other scientific disciplines.

What can human ecology do? What will it do? §1.2, "Goals and methods", deals with the subject matter of human ecology – the relationship between humans and the environment, its application in various fields of work, and the methods used in dealing with human ecology concerns.

To bridge the gap between theoretical and methodological issues, it is often useful to design and employ conceptual models. A variety of such models are scrutinized in §1.3, ranging from those with a purely biological orientation, and thus of limited validity for human ecology, to models that take social aspects into account and thus have greater relevance.

1.1 The concept and its delimitation

Environmental science – the starting point

The applied natural sciences have had some success in finding technical solutions to environmental problems – particularly air, water and soil contamination – since these problems were first brought to public attention. In the USA, environmental awareness had already begun to take hold by the mid-1960s, followed by western Europe in the late 1960s and by most of the former socialist and developing countries only after the first United Nations

Conference on the Human Environment (UNCHE) in Stockholm in 1972. The social sciences, which entered the field of environmental research even later, have also produced considerable results, for instance in the areas of environmental economics and awareness, social indicators, politico-administrative implementation and mediation between the interest groups involved. In all areas, remedial action taken against existing damage is in the foreground.

Since the oil crises in the 1970s, political pressure for the introduction of preventive measures has been increasing steadily. Among other things, this has resulted in greater emphasis being placed on basic environmental research. Examples from the natural sciences include energy use, the impacts of waste energy and ecosystem research. Basic research in the area of environment is still not prevalent among the social sciences, although some beginnings have been made. Consider, for instance, the question of social impacts of environmental policy measures or the range of theories covering everything from the social to the defensive costs of environmental protection.

It is here that the field opens up for human ecology, a basic research discipline located somewhere between the natural sciences and the social sciences. Its subject matter is the structure of the relationship between humans and nature, or society and environment. If one emphasizes the society–environment aspect, with particular reference to environmental damage as the starting point, then human ecology is primarily political ecology and, as such, its methodology will be clearly orientated towards social science, although some elements of natural science still have an important role to play. This is the concept supported here. Conversely, if one emphasizes the ecology aspect of human ecology, tying it more closely to the biological sciences, then obviously methodological elements of natural scientific study will move into the foreground of the research.

In any case, human ecology is not to be regarded as typical in the sense of conventional,compartmental university scientific research disciplines; rather, it introduces an epistemological element, an intellectual interest (Habermas: *Erkenntnisinteresse*), which tends to unify scientific disciplines. Enzensberger's critical assertion emphasizes this difference: "First of all, human ecology is a hybrid discipline in which natural and social science categories and methods must be applied concurrently, without any theoretical explanation of the resulting complications" (Enzensberger 1973: 1; see also Bruhn 1974, Young 1974). This means that the subject matter of human ecology must be defined and that adequate methods be developed. The hypothesis that nature is exploited as an economic resource provides the occasion for such innovative efforts.

From ecology to human ecology

The first definition of ecology was given in 1866 by Haeckel, a prominent German biologist (1834–1919): "Ecology is understood as the entire science of the relationships of the organism to the surrounding outside world, which, in the widest sense, can be taken to include all the conditions of existence" (Haeckel 1866: 286).[1] In his inaugural lecture in 1869, Haeckel made use of this definition of ecology as the basis for organizing the zoological sciences under one system (Haeckel, 1870: 364 f.). Here, Haeckel understands ecology to be the "science of the economic management of the faunal organism household", which investigates the "totality of an animal's relationships to its organic and inorganic surroundings"[2] and forms a branch of the "outer" or "relation physiology", which deals with the relationship of the organism to the outer world, as opposed to "inner" or "conservation physiology", which treats the functions of the organism as such, namely self-preservation, growth, nutrition and reproduction (Fig. 1.1).

Contemporary natural science ecology proceeds from the concept of biosphere, defined by E. Suess in 1875 as essentially the entire living area of organisms that inhabit the surface of the Earth.

A given section of the biosphere with all its living and non-living components is labelled an ecosystem. The size of this biospheric section is not defined. All the organisms in the world together with their environment make up one large ecosystem, the biosphere. In 1877, Möbius introduced the concept of *biocenosis* for the living part of the ecosystem, organisms in their entirety, whereas the non-living part of the ecosystem was referred to as *biotope* or habitat (Bornkamm 1971: 467).

Human ecology is a growing field of academic and practical interest. In dealing with the different relationships and interactions between humans and the environment it involves a wide variety of academic disciplines and policy fields. The growing concern in both areas of expertise is reflected in the increasing number of college and university courses, and national and international conferences on the subject.

The international conferences have taken place on an annual basis: 1989 in Scotland, 1990 in Japan, 1991 in Sweden, 1992 in the USA, 1993 in Austria and Mexico, and in 1994 and 1995 in the USA again. These conferences

---

1. "Unter Ökologie verstehen wir die gesamte Wissenschaft von den Beziehungen des Organismus zur umgebenden Außenwelt, wohin wir im weitesten Sinne alle Existenzbedingungen rechnen können."
2. "Lehre von der Ökonomie, von dem Haushalt der tierischen Organismen" welche die "gesamten Beziehungen des Tieres sowohl zu seiner anorganischen, als zu seiner organischen Umgebung zu untersuchen" hat.

4

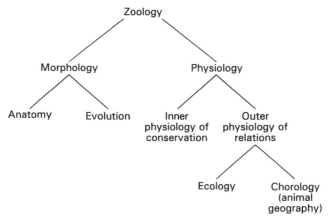

Figure 1.1 The organization of the zoological system according to Haeckel (1870).

usually combine a multitude of subjects and focus areas, and they attract academics from the natural, social and planning sciences as well as environmentalists and politicians.

More than any other human ecology society, the Commonwealth Human Ecology Council, CHEC, based in London, exerts quite a bit of political influence through its environmental and developmental work in its member countries. Through its membership and via conferences, CHEC fosters exchange between high-ranking academics, foreign diplomats and politicians, including heads of state.

Apart from CHEC, there are other national and international human ecology societies in North America, Europe, Asia (including large countries such as China, Japan and India), Latin America and Africa. The German Society for Human Ecology (DGH), to give an example, was founded in 1975 and extends its membership to include Switzerland, Austria and Belgium. The DGH holds annual workshop conferences on specific themes such as gerontecology, anxiety and the environment, lead and clean air policy, and cultural ecology. All themes are viewed from the medical, the social and planning perspectives, and range from aspects of theoretical interest to those of political implementation.

According to Wolanski (1989), the monodisciplinary approach in human ecology had given way, by the 1970s, to a multidisciplinary unidirectional perspective that focused either on human impacts on the environment or environmental impacts on human beings (Fig. 1.2). In the early 1980s a more balanced emphasis was thought to have emerged, wherein human–ecological relationships were commonly considered in both directions. Subsequently, from around 1985 onwards, the development of human ecology was considered to have reached a "transdisciplinary" stage (Wolanski 1989), characterized by integrative perspectives that effectively cut across

Stage	Year of initiation	Model	Represented by
A MONODISCIPLINARY	1921	$T \rightarrow M;\ N \rightarrow M;\ C \rightarrow M$ etc.	Separate doctrines in each related discipline
B1 MULTIDISCIPLINARY (mosaic, in sciences)	c. 1972	 T N C ↓ ↓ ↓etc. M M M / T N C |/etc. Man	"Certificate in human ecology" of several west European universities: Geneva, Brussels, etc.
B2 MULTIDISCIPLINARY (mosaic, in engineering)	c. 1975	M M M ↓ ↓ ↓etc. T N C / Man /|\etc. T N C	International Organization for Human Ecology, Vienna
B3 MULTIDISCIPLINARY (mosaic, reversible)	c. 1980	T N C ↓ ↓ ↓etc. M M M / Man /|\etc. T N C	Society for Human Ecology, USA
C TRANSDISCIPLINARY	c. 1985	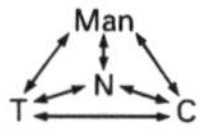 Man /↕\ T ⟷ N ⟷ C	Commission of Human Ecology IUAES

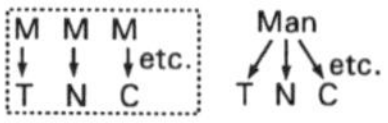

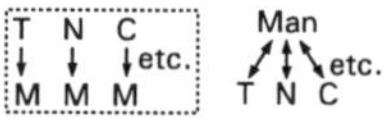

T climate (temperature, etc.)
N nutrition (food, nutritional customs, etc.)
C culture (education, income, organizations, man-made environment, etc.)
M man (organism, population, society)

Figure 1.2 Stages of development of scientific human ecology.
Source: Wolanski (1989).

disciplinary boundaries. However, this tendency, if it is real, may not be general. Whereas research with a transdisciplinary perspective existed in the early 1970s (e.g. Forrester 1971a), human ecological work with a multidisciplinary unidirectional perspective still prevails in the 1990s (e.g. Friday & Laskey 1991).

Nevertheless, the capacity to examine relationships across disciplines is developing and it appears to be associated with a broadening focus. The intra-relationships *within* human and environmental elements, respectively, are now being examined in addition to the interrelationships *between* them, especially in problem-orientated human ecological research (e.g. Adekayi et al. 1990).

Yet the human ecological approach, whatever its disciplinary status, continued to be regarded as necessary both for an understanding of complex human and environmental problems and because of human dependency on ecological interactions and organizational structures. According to Borden (1989), it was during the 1980s that the human ecological approach finally became established, having followed a difficult path strewn with false starts. By the end of that decade human ecology had its own framework of transdisciplinary concepts, focusing on the process of *interaction*, based largely on theory and research in biological ecology (Young 1989). "The incorporation of knowledge in an *applied* human ecological perspective" was identified as *the* remaining challenge (Borden 1989: 142). Certainly this is one challenge for contemporary human ecologists; another is the development of an *integrative* methodology.

The human ecology approach in the academic disciplines

The term "human ecology" was developed as a supplementary specification, analogous to plant ecology and animal ecology. Human ecology is distinct from biological ecology in that human ecology deals with the "special relationships that exist between humans and their environment" (Bornkamm 1971: 468 f.). Special human–environment relations under the heading of human ecology have already been investigated and described in terms of biological, anthropo-geographical, psychological and sociological aspects (Fig. 1.3). The transdisciplinary nature of human ecology is illustrated in Figure 1.4.

BIOLOGY
According to Bornkamm, one problem of the ecology concept (ecology as the science of the relationships of all organisms to their environment) lies in the fact that although humans are undoubtedly organisms, is it enough to leave it at that? "Are human beings to be placed on equal footing with other organisms in terms of ecology? Should humans be regarded as environmental factors or are they to be attributed special status as conscious, purposeful shapers of the ecosystem?" The answer is that in the course of its prehistoric and historic appearance, the human species has demonstrated the ability to actively influence the biosphere and, in so doing, has developed "from being

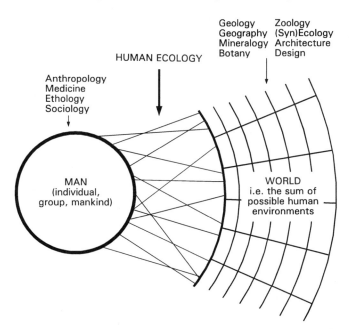

Figure 1.3   Human ecology. *Source:* IOHE (1981).

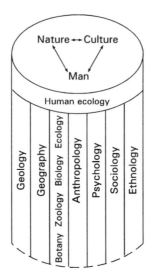

Figure 1.4 The transdisciplinary nature of human ecology.
Source: Wolanski (1989).

a member of certain ecosystems to being a partner in almost all ecosystems. Those attributes we like to regard as being specifically human – soul, mind [*Geist*], the use of tools, speech, the construction of symbols – are the cause of the unique position human beings occupy among the organisms" (Bornkamm 1971: 468). During the course of technical development, new biocenoses and anthropogenic biotopes were created, and with them emerged new ecosystems.

GEOGRAPHY

Schröter's observations focus on the relationship between biology and geography. He defined "ecological plant geography" demecologically as "the ecology of the individual species themselves in relation to their geographic dissemination" and, on the other hand, synecologically as the "ecology of plant societies" based on the following criteria: "ecological conditions of location, [and] the ecology of formation constituents, genesis, conditions for preservation and changes in the formations" (Schröter & Kirchner 1902: 64 f.).

Environmental research based on geographic elements had been introduced earlier by Hellpach's *Geopsyche*, which dealt with "spiritual life in so far as it is affected and thus altered by weather or climate, soil or landscape" (Hellpach 1950 [1911]: 4). For over half a century, Hellpach saw his geopsychology as "the only systematically prepared source for observations and documentation of nature's influence on experience and behaviour" (Graumann 1972: 1235) – in the context of a psychology of the environment. This comprehensive approach was only carried on, however, in separate camps by geographers and psychologists under the headings of "landscape" and "behaviour". Only in recent times has the idea of functional unity between landscape and behaviour, i.e. mutual interaction and dependency of humans and nature, regained attention in the form of a new paradigm, behavioural geography.

PSYCHOLOGY

In the field of psychology, Craik began working on environmental psychology that proceeded from landscape. According to Craik, work in the area of human ecology implies the study of the entire system of relations between persons, other organisms and the physical environment; thus human behaviour must be interpreted in terms of the whole ecosystem of which humans are a part and to which their behaviour relates functionally (Craik 1970: 47). According to this view, human ecology is characterized less as a specific scientific discipline and more as an aspect of human behaviour.

Accordingly, the main object of research in the North American environmental psychology tradition, which also labels itself "human ecology", is the physical–spatial environment – including the geographical and urban environment as well as the niches and corners of a house – and its influence on individual human behaviour. Most empirical studies are limited to spatial and temporal distribution of day-to-day behavioural phenomena such as those in psychiatric hospitals, student residences, libraries and residential areas. The three essential variables in this are:
- activities or behaviour patterns
- the related spatiality, and
- the persons under observation.

SOCIOLOGY

Social ecology, which first appeared in 1921 in the work of Park & Burgess, was regarded as a method of ecological observation of human society, primarily of urbanization. The first "tentative", formal definition of human ecology in the sense of social ecology was provided by McKenzie in 1924/5: ". . . a study of the spatial and temporal relations of human beings as affected by the selective, distributive and accommodative forces of the environment" (McKenzie 1925: 63 f.). The influence of plant and animal ecology can still be detected here. Since Hawley (1944, 1950), social ecology has been interpreted as the study of the form and development of the human community. Areas of empirical research include zoning in large cities, spatial distribution of slum populations, residential working-class areas, and detached single-family houses; they may also include urban partitioning according to land use, for instance, in business, industrial and residential areas. Other areas of research include population size, the most important variable after space, and the expansion of conurbations into surrounding areas.

From the medical paradigm to human ecology

Environmental pollution provides the occasion for human ecological research. It is a disruptive incident, an abnormal situation that forces us to pause and reconsider some of the "regular relations" among observable things. This concept is modelled after the medical paradigm, according to which health can only be defined in terms of illness. Medical abnormalities, the "disruptive incidents", occasioned the development of physiology as a theory of the organism, and of medicine as a policy towards organisms. This applies threefold:

- historically, as motive and stimulus to investigate the "normal case"
- systematically, as an instrument for determining the normal case
  e contrario, from its opposite
- politically and practically, as an explanation for the social relevance of
  theoretical human ecology constructs.

Prevention in medical terms means taking appropriate measures early to protect health. Primary prevention implies avoidance of the circumstances in which illness can occur, and it includes, for instance, environmental protection measures to prevent environmental damage that could ultimately contribute to ill health. Secondary prevention aims at preventing the disease itself (the course of which is already known) from developing. Tertiary prevention is designed to hinder relapse. Preventative measures are thus dependent upon:

- the end in view, i.e. the definition of the goal and the degree of health
  provide the norm
- a definition of illness, i.e. the cause, effects and side-effects
- the possibilities for therapy, i.e. the spectrum of therapeutic and pro-
  phylactic measures in so far as different measures come under consideration.

The instrument of human medicine, as regards definition and implementation, can now be transferred broadly to the concept of environmental policy. In place of the human organism, however, we are now dealing with the environment in the sense of the ecosystem or the biosphere. Environmental ends, definitions of environmental damage and the array of strategies for dealing with them only make sense in this analogy if they are taken as a whole. As in the practice of medicine, in environmental policy it is not always a simple task to distinguish between causes and symptoms, and to design an appropriate therapy. One example of this is the case of forest dieback. Another example is the so-called "sick-building syndrome", the causes of which are not known but whose effects or symptoms are observable: there are buildings in which people simply do not feel well, in which they suffer constantly recurring illnesses, other disturbances or distress.

From the viewpoint of medicine, the separation of the individual from the environment is a basic phylogenetic principle. In humans, the skin constitutes the "demarcation line". Every human action can be interpreted as a reaction to this fact; the stimulus for all behaviour results from the separation that exists between the individuals and their environments. Arising from the tension caused by this separation, human ecology provides an integrative and holistic approach that seeks to perceive the interplay between human beings and the environment as a system that can possibly be influenced.

1.2 Goals and methods

Given the great variety of traditions that belong to the domain of human ecology in its concern with the complex relationship between humans and their environment, it is questionable as to whether the quality of this broad spectrum can be apprehended.

The natural science approach is at least aware of the sociopolitical components, although understandably it does not deal with them adequately. Social science research, on the other hand, is constantly dealing with "environment" as an independent variable in contrast to the types of behaviour dependent on it, without specifically being concerned with feedback. The result is that environment is treated as a static quantity.[3] The objection can be raised here, of course, that the environmental concepts used do not have much in common, since some are concerned exclusively with natural environments and natural phenomena, whereas others deal with social environments and social phenomena. Nevertheless, this distinction is itself indicative of the lack of awareness of existing interrelations.

Thus, it is not a new scientific discipline with unique content that is being sought; rather, the aim is to find a theoretical structure whose methodology is adequate and appropriate for dealing with social dependencies, environmental relationships, and their repercussions on the environment itself. In so doing, consideration must be given specifically to natural–social environment correlations.

Object of cognition

The International Organization for Human Ecology (IOHE) in Vienna defines human ecology as follows: that which deals "with human life in all its physical, chemical, biotic, mental, social, and cultural manifestations from an ecological point of view; this means considering the interrelationships of a human being or several human beings and the outside world surrounding

---

3. The transformation of the landscape, a central theme in geography, constitutes an important exception.

him/her or them" (IOHE 1981). The IOHE believes that human ecology should proceed from Haeckel's definition of ecology as the "ecology of the species *Homo sapiens*". The science of the interrelations among living beings and their surrounding world manifests itself as a systemic science. Interrelations and interactions depend on the traits of those affected, on the one hand, and the characteristics of the surrounding world, on the other. Human ecology is understood to be one of several special ecologies, namely, that of humans. The specific difference is that "human beings are capable of purposive action and of understanding the functioning of systems of which they are part" (IOHE 1981).

Human ecology in the sense of political ecology, which has a stronger social science orientation, puts greater emphasis on the human social context as well as politically and economically motivated human action and behaviour. Accordingly, "human" environment implies first and foremost the societal production spheres, essentially areas of agriculture and industry. Both these spheres of production can be described as input–output systems controlled by human societies for the exploitation of nature. Renewable and non-renewable resources such as energy, raw materials, minerals, or soil fertility enter into the system as input. After various transformation processes, industrial and agricultural products emerge as output along with by-products such as waste, heat or hazardous substances. The consequences and side-effects of these production processes went less noticed in the past, but they are now gaining in importance as potential sources of crises. On the input side, this means resource exhaustion through raw material extraction or soil depletion. Negative effects on the output end include adverse impacts on the ecological balance of nature. In short, the human being – nature interaction finds its ultimate expression in overexploitation of natural resources and the plundering and destruction of nature by society with the aid of the organized system of production.

This system of natural exploitation is not limited to appropriating natural resources as a factor of production, however; it also has to employ human labour power as yet another factor in the transformation process. The human producer enters into the process of nature exploitation as an expendable and renewable resource as well.

Therefore, the question of utilization of nature, including the exploitation of humans by humans, within and among the economic sectors of industry and agriculture as well as between the North and the South on a worldwide scale, must be put to critical scrutiny. The practical appropriation of nature must be studied in terms of underlying economic and historical conditions, based on a theory of social action that concerns the utilization of nature. It is especially important here to work out the structural and historical correlations in human–nature relationships within the physical environment, and in human–human relationships within the social environment.

Proceeding on the basis of empirically derived human ecological patterns of relationships, it is then necessary to inquire into the cognitive relations between humans and environment, that is working from a theory of action, to investigate the practical conditions underlying theoretical exploitation of nature. To the extent to which we alter nature in the course of production, we also become more aware of it. Cognition in terms of production means ". . . that we recognize an object only to the extent that we can create it ourselves" (Habermas 1967: 14, after Giambattista Vico 1924 [1744]; see also Eder 1988: 15–16).

Investigations into human ecological interaction as production and production as cognition fall within the framework of social science. The first delves into the metabolic processes between humans and nature. Similarities between the utilization of human labour power and the exploitation of natural resources are of special interest. The question is posed as to whether an historical correlation can be found, for instance, between ecological and economic exploitation processes based on industrialized production methods and colonialism, or the problems of developing countries. If this proves to be the case, then it is reasonable to assume that structural similarities exist. A structural correspondence could be made transparent, for instance, using production theory based on the labour–commodity concept. Can an analogy be drawn between the way labour and the environment are treated as production factors?

The study of production as cognition can be thought of as a "metascience". It deals with the question of the structural identity of action and cognition. Objects of experience are recognizable to the extent that they are human products or that they can be altered through human actions, that is, created under historical conditions – for instance, through natural science experiments, industrial production methods or social processes. To what extent is work the foundation not only for behavioural interaction, but also cognitive interaction between humans and the environment, thereby itself forming a category of action-orientated cognition? Theory itself, as a product of the way in which nature is exploited, is at issue here. Answering these questions is essential to resolving the current exploitation conflict between society and environment. Does the alternative, co-operative utilization, as opposed to exploitative utilization of nature, coincide with parallel transformations going on in the scientific process? The question of a shift in awareness and changing social values forms the connecting link here.

The holistic concept of human ecology

The concept of wholeness and the ideas of holistic thought are – once again – enjoying wide popularity. Is this just a fad, or could there be something of more lasting meaning to it than it would at first appear? In order to answer this question, we must first ask ourselves:

- What do we mean by wholeness?
- What role has holistic thought played historically?
- What is the significance of wholeness in environmental protection?

When we say wholeness we mean the characteristics of things or systems that display a "qualitatively distinct and autonomous behaviour with respect to their constituent parts" (Klaus & Buhr 1976: 443). Concepts such as completeness, intactness and autonomy are relevant here. Thus it is necessary to distinguish between "wholeness" and "totality": *wholeness*, the whole, is a *qualitative* definition, whereas *totality* (entirety) is a *quantitative* composition made up of a certain number of elements or parts.

This distinction – and here we combine the question of wholeness with a few historical remarks – can be traced back to Aristotle, who clearly separated *holon* (whole) and *pan* (totality) (*Metaphysics*, 1023b/1024a). Thus the repeated *dictum* of Aristotelian metaphysics that the whole is more than the sum of its parts must be understood qualitatively, not quantitatively. It means that the relationship between the parts cannot be derived from laws that apply to the *individual* parts, but only from the whole. Underlying this principle is the consideration that cross-system interrelations *cannot* be extrapolated and interpreted from partial areas; the opposite is true: only when a system's coherence is fully understood can partial areas be classified, hence known.

Such considerations have played a role in a wide variety of disciplines in the natural and social sciences. Although an "archaeology of sciences" could be pursued in this respect, the following are just a few examples of what might be included:

- the unified concept of the world in physics
- vitalism in biology and physiology
- the holistic psychology of the 1920s
- the structural and functional approach to society in sociology and cultural anthropology
- reading and writing instruction in elementary education.

Holistic thinking currently finds its most widespread expression in ecology and human ecology. It can be said that the popularity these fields of science enjoy is due precisely to the fact that in their structures they satisfy a widely felt need for holistic thought. This need contrasts sharply not only with the destruction of the environment, which can be seen occurring everywhere, but also with current agricultural and development policy, which reacts only selectively, partially and in belated response to the symptoms of environmental destruction; in other words, it is anything but holistic or sustainable.

Let us summarize the preceding: according to the considerations given above, holistic agricultural and development policy would have to fulfil the following requirements:

- It would have to be possible to generate it within the context of specific independence and autonomy, *quasi* from an inherent principle.
- Its parts or its applications in sectoral policy (in industry, agriculture, health care) would have to be derivable from – or at least understandable in terms of – this principle and not the reverse.
- Its norms would have to be compatible with the natural and sociocultural environments in which it is embedded.

The central *thesis* of this volume is then that sustainable agricultural policy can be developed within the framework of concepts that are henceforth formulated as the basis of human ecology.

From the viewpoint of science, one specific ecology would be that of the species *Homo sapiens*, i.e. human ecology. From the viewpoint of social science, the human being – as expressed in Aristotelian terms – is not only a *zoon logon echon*, or an animal capable of reason, but a *zoon politikon*, i.e. a living social being as well, one whose interactions with nature are socially determined, such as by technical and economic, but also by scientific and cultural processes. These processes have led to the degradation and exploitation, the exhaustion and weakening of external nature, so that ultimately the portent of the end of the very basis of human life has become a distinct historical possibility.

This is where conventional environmental policy steps in, mostly concerned with belated, partial repair of environmental damage (Glaeser 1988). Human ecology plays a role here, too: by providing a theoretical basis for a holistic, preventive environmental policy (Glaeser 1989a).

Human ecology takes interactive processes in the relationship between nature and society as the basis for defining the structure of environmental destruction. It uses the same approach to prepare a unified basis upon which to formulate environmental policy in accordance with guiding principles. The environmental policy is holistic in the sense of the above-mentioned criteria when the human ecological basis possesses an autonomy that binds the natural and sociocultural environments to one another and from which parts such as an environmentally orientated departmental policy can be generated.

Methodology

Holistic thinking, the integrative approach, and the paradigmatic treatment of case studies are regarded as the methodological mainstays of human ecology. All three principles are interdeterminant: none may be isolated within nor extracted from the basic methodological framework. The decisive factor is a problem-orientated approach, which deals with issues from various specialized scientific perspectives. This type of approach is necessary because every interaction *between* humans and nature implies a complete interaction framework that can have different facets, and overlapping between different areas of scientific investigation.

This approach also sheds some light on the relationship between general and specialized human ecology. As specialization in human ecology increases, one must wonder whether there is a real danger of fragmentation, since it is only with some difficulty that the various specific human ecologies can be reduced to a common denominator. On the other hand, the existence of specialized human ecologies in the sense of applied human ecologies is justified by the methodological argument: they can be taken as case studies and treated as paradigms, thus contributing to the feedback process that enhances and deepens our general understanding of human ecology.

This aim is well served by the so-called integrative approach, because it combines the general with the specific, putting them in a mutually complementary context. On the one hand, the theory directs and guides the cognition of the examples; on the other hand, it is empirically confirmed or refuted by such examples.

Both effects depend solely on a flexible methodology. The integrative approach theoretically permits use and adoption of experiences and methods across scientific disciplines. The reason for this lies in the complex relationship between humans and nature, or society and environment, which extends from economic–technical environmental intervention through scientific experimentation to forms of perception in the field of aesthetics or normative behaviour in the field of ethics.

Scientific reflection must be methodologically capable of dealing with this degree of complexity. This occurs in cases of societal relevance with the use of economic and social science instruments, further supplemented, as the need arises, by the methods and techniques of cybernetics, systems analysis, biology and physics.

This means that in human ecology the gap between the social and natural sciences cannot be bridged using formal criteria: rather, this will occur in substance through experience. Returning to the issue of paradigms, the general problem of processes and structures between society and the environment will thus be dealt with on a case-by-case basis. This means that from the perspective of sociology, economics and ecology, empirically documented cases of interaction with the environment – for instance, the environmental repercussions of industrial production, agricultural production, or the exploitation of natural resources in the Third World – will be analyzed accordingly. Returning to the theoretical level, on the basis of one or several such cases, common structures will be derived for human–nature relations. The conceptual "pivot points" for this sort of process will be concepts such as "goods" or "labour". The theoretical aim of such a process could, among other things, include the conceptual and, in some cases, ideologically critical formulation of possible "imbalances" in ecology, economy and society. Such a programme represents one of many possible approaches social science can take to theory formulation in human ecology. The relationship to ecology is revealed bit by bit, strengthened by selected paradigms, when the "bridge" is constructed from individual cases back to general theory.

1.3 Conceptual models in human ecology

The achievement of integration and holism in human ecological studies are daunting tasks, for many diverse variables must be considered, and large gaps in knowledge exist. Special tools are needed to provide a framework against which studies can be organized. Frequently, conceptual models are constructed for this purpose. These are abstract and often schematic representations of perceived human ecological systems. According to Boyden (1979: 19) such a model should:

> provide the basis for the selection of variables for study, for the consideration of patterns of interplay between the different components of the system, for the formulation and testing of hypotheses concerning dynamic interrelationships within the system, and for communication at all levels of education and specialism.

A conceptual model may also help in the identification of data inadequacies and gaps in knowledge (e.g. Frissel 1977). When used in applied studies, such a model may aid the location of "pressure points" at which the system may be sensitive as well as "structural constraints" on possible problem solutions (Clapham 1980: 151).

Nevertheless, as Ellen (1982) points out: obfuscation due to complexity and reduction to algebraic and graphic conventions should be avoided; there may be a tendency to emphasize the static character of systems without conveying the extent to which they are changing; and, such modelling is part of an analysis that may portray unforeseen relationships and eliminate detail.

Perhaps the greatest non-technical problem is to be aware of the value judgements that enter, often unintentionally, into the modelling decisions that are made. These may be particularly significant when they result in the neglect or obscuration of important variables, components or relationships. This problem seems to be particularly great with respect to biologically orientated models, which are often assumed to be "value-free". However, as Friedland (1977: 119) observed:

> It is a methodological fact of life that no matter how sincerely a model builder may aspire to creating "value-free" models and no matter how scrupulously he adheres to that goal, he cannot. His own notions of

purpose and value will necessarily enter into all the modelling choices he must make.

Despite the acknowledged problems of model-building, the development of a meaningful and useful conceptual model is, according to Boyden (1979: 11), one of the most essential tasks facing human ecologists. We dispute the point that a single, universally applicable, model should be sought because, as Weichhart (1979) clearly demonstrated, time and space scales, types of environments, levels of aggregation, directions of impacts and modes of relations may all differ from one study to another. However, the need to construct and improve conceptual models is clearly worthwhile for the scientific advancement of the subject. Here the intention is to contribute to this process by means of a critical, comparative analysis of various models developed over the past two decades.

Biologically orientated models

To many workers in this field, human ecology involves the extension of ecological methodology, as developed in the biological sciences, to study the interrelationships between human beings and their environments (e.g. Barrows 1923, Bews 1935, Dice 1955, Eyre & Jones 1966, Sargent 1974, Levine 1975).

This view is clearly exemplified in the model (Fig. 1.5) devised by Worthington (1973) to illustrate the scope of human ecology.

Figure 1.5 places human beings at the top of a network of trophic relationships between animals, plants and the non-living components of the natural

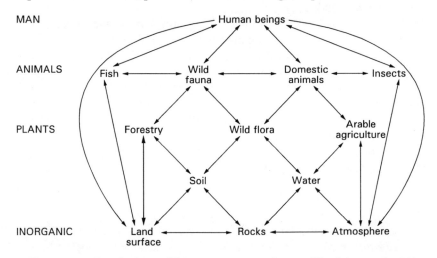

Figure 1.5 Rural man and his environment. *Source:* Worthington (1973).

environment. This model is noteworthy because of the way in which it emphasizes the dependence of human beings on their biophysical environment, a point generally ignored by social scientists who have adhered to the "human exemptionalist paradigm" (Dunlap 1980: 6). The arrows represent channels of energy flow associated with conversions of matter from one form to another. The whole network is regarded as an ecosystem, and "rural man" is the top consumer.

The limitations of this model, acknowledged by its designer, are that it is applicable more to the rural than to the urban setting, and that it should include reversible arrows between human beings and all other components. However, the notion that human beings can be regarded simply as a component of a closed biophysical ecosystem was not questioned. This implies that people are trophic units like animals and plants, that their behaviour is passive, and that their lives are constrained by the laws of thermodynamics and locally available natural resources. It overlooks the vitally important point that all human relationships, including those with nature, are characterized by purposeful social action (cf. Glaeser 1980). Human purposes – such as the achievement of production targets, higher living standards, larger profits, security and survival – being products of cognition, represent a unique and potentially powerful source of ecological dynamism. When translated into action, in the context of society, human purposes can simplify, destabilize and otherwise transform the structure and function of ecosystems. Hence, many ecosystems may be regarded as biophysical manifestations of realized human purposes.

It would be reasonable, therefore, to take account of human behavioural adaptation, that is, the coping mechanisms displayed by human beings in obtaining their wants, in adjusting their lives to the surrounding milieu, and in modifying the milieu to suit their lives and purposes (Bennett 1976: 246). This implies that the socio-economic, psychological, political and legal factors that influence adaptive decisions should be included in conceptual models for human ecology. A report prepared by Delft Hydraulics Laboratory (1981), which was orientated towards decision-makers, subscribes to this view by asserting that such factors strongly influence all decisions affecting ambient environmental quality.

With respect to the above, the model shown in Figure 1.5 does not adequately illustrate the scope of human ecology. It is obviously inapplicable to urban industrial areas, but also to undeveloped rural areas. This is because, apart from its other deficiencies, the model represents "rural settings" as closed systems, that is systems without any external contacts or trade.

Some of the deficiencies of Worthington's model are partially overcome in the model (Fig. 1.6) devised by Newbould (1973), which at least acknowledges the relevance of external determinants. This model emphasizes the role of "Technological Man" and specifies certain interactions (exchanges of energy, minerals and information) that involve human beings.

19

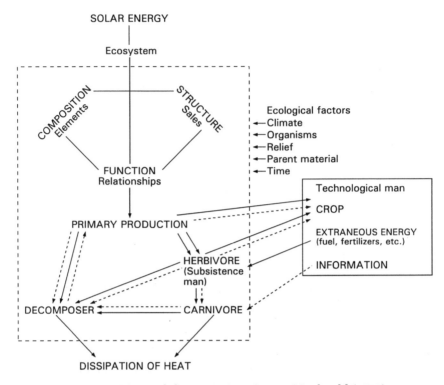

Figure 1.6 Man and the ecosystem. *Source:* Newbould (1973).

Nevertheless, Newbould's model also has a strong and, from a social science viewpoint, unrealistic biological orientation. "Technological Man" is regarded simply as an external factor (albeit a powerful one) that interacts with the production processes of a fundamentally natural ecosystem, and the human determinants of adaptive behaviour are omitted. This model was proposed as a tolerable starting point for descriptive and comparative ecological studies of human communities, although Newbould expressed doubts about the applicability of the ecosystem concept to urban situations.

However, there are many problems in attempting to apply the ecosystem concept in human ecology, especially to urban and contemporary economic settings; although, according to Young (1989), this is still worth pursuing. Conversely, Bennett (1976) argued that the ecosystem concept can rarely, if ever, be appropriate for human ecological studies because it implies automatic feedback control (as opposed to societal control) of man–environment interactions.

This feedback problem is illustrated here with respect to the ecosystem-watershed model (Fig. 1.7) that was applied by O'Sullivan (1979) to interpret the trophic history of Lough Neagh, Northern Ireland. According to O'Sulli-van (1979: 279–280), feedback in the form of algal blooms (which were attrib-

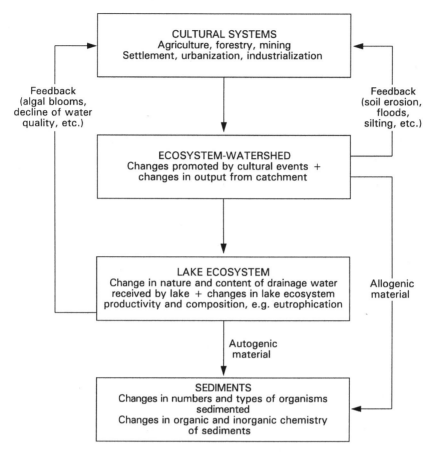

Figure 1.7 Relationship between cultural systems and sediments in ecosystem watersheds. *Source:* O'Sullivan (1979).

uted to high phosphorus loadings from domestic sewage) resulted in the decision to install a phosphorus-reducing plant at the major sewage works draining into Lough Neagh.

This interpretation assumes that the monitoring of phosphorus loadings was reliable and that the decision involved no "human" factors. However, Phillips-Howard (1982) showed that the monitoring was systematically biased, maximizing the phosphorus contributions attributed to the sewage works (and the rural population) and minimizing those from land drainage. Moreover, it appeared that the decision reflected a concern to protect agricultural interests. It was suggested that the "results of feedback" were inappropriate, in that phosphorus reduction at the major sewage works, without any limitation on land drainage sources, would not effectively control the eutrophication of Lough Neagh.

For the phosphorus reduction decision to be fully understood, it was suggested that a thorough analysis of the institutional context and the relevant socio-economic factors was needed. Even so, it is clear that the feedback process was not simple, not automatic, and certainly not analogous to that observed in biological ecosystems.

Energy-flow models, derived from studies of natural ecosystems, have been extensively adapted and applied in studying human situations. The pioneering work in this field, by Odum (1971), argued that "power" (the rate of flow of useful energy), being the common denominator of natural and socio-economic processes, provides a quantitative measure for integrative, "macroscopic" studies of the relations between man and nature. Odum and his co-workers have developed procedures whereby flows of energy, matter, goods, services and money can all be equated. These have been applied in a variety of regional models (e.g. Zucchetto 1975, Hall & Day 1977, Jansson 1980), an example of which is shown in Figure 1.8.

Such models could be of considerable value as descriptive tools that clearly demonstrate some of the connections between human and natural systems. Moreover, information on energy patterns could provide a useful measure of human activity in an area, and have important human and environmental implications (e.g. Boyden 1979: 39).

Nevertheless, energy-based models do involve simplistic, and sometimes forced, reduction of complex relationships into flows of joules or calories.

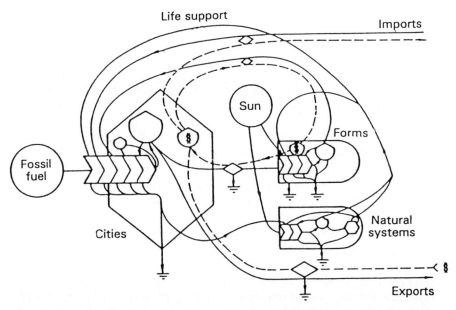

Figure 1.8 General system diagram for energy basis for a country aggregated into urban, agricultural and environmental components. *Source:* Odum (1977).

They inevitably favour processes that are readily quantified over those such as "social power" (Bennett & Chorley 1978) that are not, and often exhibit greater fascination with modelling techniques *per se* than with the subject under investigation. Also, being based on physical principles, these models represent a human ecological system as a clock-like mechanism devoid of human spontaneity and meaning. Such energy-based models also divert attention from vitally important socio-economic considerations (such as attitudes, motives, goals, interests and sources of control) while contributing little to our knowledge of how and why sociosystems and ecosystems interact as they do.

Similarly, models of nutrient flow could also be useful as aids for the description of human ecological relationships. In particular, they could be relevant for understanding the sources, distribution and losses of materials, especially food (Fig. 1.9).

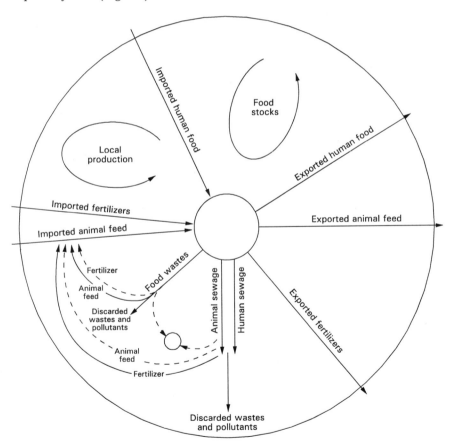

Figure 1.9 A schematic representation of nutrient flow in the Hong Kong food system. *Source:* Newcombe (1977).

The development and application of such models could provide valuable information for decision-makers concerned with resource conservation and waste management (Friend 1978). Moreover, in the case of cities, the balance between nutrient inputs and outputs may allow per capita consumption, a comparative measure of nutritional health, to be calculated (Newcombe 1977).

However, nutrient-based models share many of the limitations of energy-based models. They too are often mechanistic: human systems are represented as huge feedlots and human beings as biological production units, like hens on a factory farm. Complex socio-economic processes are reduced, for example, to flows of nitrogen and phosphorus. Moreover, because such calculations involve large errors (especially for nutrients like nitrogen that may exist in a gaseous phase), the results may have relative validity only.

If nutrient and energy-flow models are to be significant and useful in the context of human ecology, their development and application should take full account of the socio-economic determinants of human activity.

The same applies to models for environmental studies, because most environments are now modified, if not dominated, by human action. Such human dominance indicates that explanations of trends in ecosystem behaviour should be sought primarily in human behaviour (Phillips-Howard 1985), and that models of the latter should be superimposed on those of the former.

For example, Figure 1.10 is an illustration of the problem-chain approach for studying agricultural impacts on water quality, developed by Clapham & Pestel (1978). The problem chain originates with management activities that are listed on the left. These activities are conceived as the products of decisions by individual farmers, which are influenced by policies, other actors, institutions, laws and ultimately by social values and goals. The problem-chain approach is exemplary among biologically orientated models for representing complex systems simply and efficiently without great loss of structure, dynamism or realism.

Biological ecology conforms with the traditions of positivism and logical empiricism that characterize Western natural science. Accordingly, it is concerned with observable, verifiable facts and claims to be value-free; but, as many social scientists agree, such an approach cannot be realistically applied to human situations. Investigators' notions of good and bad, and of right and wrong, as well as those pertaining to their cultural background, readily enter into modelling decisions. This is particularly obvious with instrumental values, which, according to Skolimowski (1981: 59), become pre-eminent in the absence of any set of intrinsic values.

With respect to biologically orientated models, it appears that biophysicochemical objects, processes and transformations do seem to be highly valued. To Worthington, Newbould and many other ecologists, environmental conservation and the functional integrity of ecosystems matter most for the survival of our species. Odum and co-workers are apparently concerned

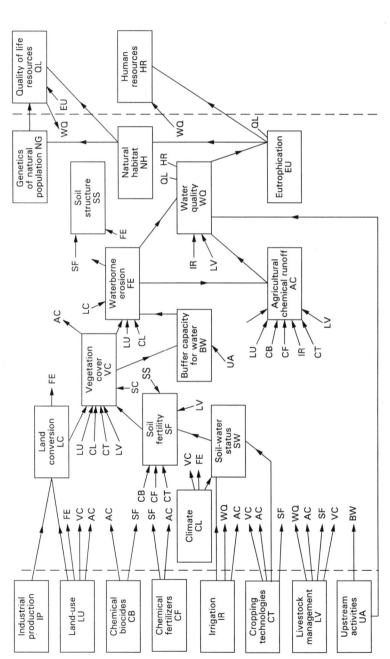

Figure 1.10 Construction of problem chains focused on agricultural water pollution. *Source:* Clapham & Pestel (1978).

more about the mechanisms of energy flow and how to manage them, whereas the maintenance of biological nutrient cycles, frugal resource use and the maximum sustainability of material flows are particularly important to the proponents of nutrient-based models (e.g. Borgstrom 1973, Newcombe 1977, Friend 1978).

Such values invest biologically orientated models with an instrumental imperative, which translated into action becomes a narrow, "technological imperative" (Skolimowski 1981: 79). Consequently, narrow "technical" solutions are invariably proposed for problems that also have socio-economic, political and psychological dimensions.

The conscious exclusion of human values (such as equity, co-operation, risk aversion and livelihood security) suggests that they are unimportant. This "value-free" stance has distinctive and self-defeating political implications, which are often not recognized. In the context of management, it serves the interests of the status quo and thereby the continuation of exploitative and destructive behaviour towards human beings and their environments. Hence, for human ecological models to be meaningful, they should also be normative, or at least have their values made more explicit.

Finally, it is noted that biologically orientated models cannot be regarded as holistic in the context of human ecology. Holism requires the ecologists' frequent insistence upon the essential biological nature of human ecology (e.g. Worthington 1973: 12) to be relinquished. It is beyond question that Haeckel's original definition of the subject (quoted earlier) can fully accommodate the distinctly human aspects of human ecology. Indeed, because the *human being* has unique somatic, psychological and extrasomatic characteristics, and because its *"surrounding outer world"* includes anthropogenic social, economic, ideological and cultural components (e.g. Bennett & Chorley 1978, Weichhart 1979), the whole science of the relationships between the two *must* consider these aspects if it is to be realistic and meaningful. Accordingly, conceptual models that incorporate social science perspectives are regarded as potentially more appropriate than biologically orientated ones as a basis for human ecological studies.

Socially orientated models

Various conceptual models have been devised that attempt to incorporate social science orientations into human ecology. Among the simplest of the social-science–inclusive models are the "dualistic" ones, which conceive of human beings and their environments as two distinct interacting entities. The IOHE (1981) general model in Figure 1.3 represents man as a circle, the world as a surrounding ring, and the subject matter of human ecology as the set of links between them. Each link is perforce two-ended, and the two ends are regarded as equally important to the whole.

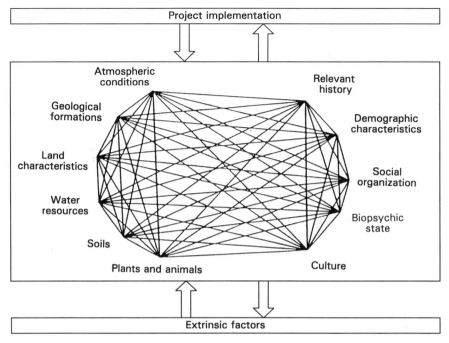

Figure 1.11 Interactions of development projects with the man–environment system. *Source:* Phillips-Howard (1985).

Social science perspectives are introduced when, using the "integrative approach" the links are considered from the human as well as from the environmental end. The IOHE states that "it is a *conditio sine qua non* [for human ecology] to pay absolutely equal attention to the work of both the natural and the social sciences" (IOHE 1981: 1). This condition seems to be inspired by the dualism of the model; it is apparently not based on knowledge of how people actually interact with their environments. An important limitation of the IOHE model is that it apparently excludes consideration of interrelationships within the human and environmental subsections. It thereby makes the explanation of man–environment relationships virtually impossible.

A more inclusive dualistic model is shown in Figure 1.11. This was devised by Phillips-Howard (1985) specifically for studying the local human and environmental impacts of large-scale development projects. It takes account of historical, sociopolitical and psychological factors and, under the heading of "culture", includes economic, technological, legal and ideological factors.

In contrast to the previous model, this one accepts the importance for human ecology of relationships within human and environmental components. Moreover, it includes the relevant "extrinsic factors" (mainly socioeconomic) as well as interactions relating to "project implementation". Yet

27

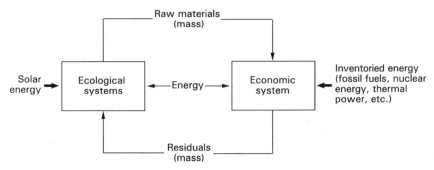

Figure 1.12 Material and energy flows in ecosystems and the economic system. *Source:* Wilen (1973).

this model appears excessively complex, and has limited potential because it is concerned more with taxonomy than with the dynamic processes involved, and it fails to focus on the sources of control. The main value explicitly associated with the model in Figure 1.11 is a concern for socio-economic development without destructive human or environmental repercussions.

Another type of dualistic model, which was devised by Wilen (1973), is represented in its schematic form in Figure 1.12. This model focuses specifically on economic system–ecosystem interactions, but it is not intended to be holistic. It is based on the material-balance model of Ayres & Kneese (1969) and involves equations that describe inputs, outputs and exchanges of raw materials, energy and wastes.

This model has great potential for studies of the production relationships central to man–environment interactions (e.g. Glaeser 1980). It could be used as a core for human ecological studies and expanded to include the social, political and ecological factors, and the control sources that influence economic and biological production.

As it stands, however, the model is biased towards physical (material) and quantitative interactions and is distinctly mechanistic. Other problems associated with this model are: the assumptions of fixed coefficients; the exclusion of point production interdependencies and synergistic effects; the static nature of the analysis (Wilen 1973: 420), and its supposed value-free stance.

The last dualistic model to be considered here (Fig. 1.13) is an early geographical one. Man is conceived as an organism that interacts with the biophysical environment directly and by way of intervening variables. The latter (culture, perception and behaviour) can be considered to include the relevant social, economic, psychological, political and technological factors.

However, the notion of intervention implies that these factors simply modify man–environment interactions in a subordinate or incidental way. The possibility that certain intervening variables may actually be a source of action is overlooked. Furthermore, this model describes a closed system,

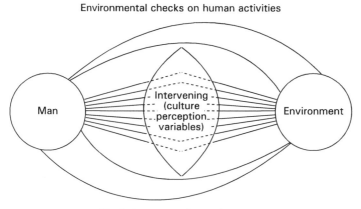

Figure 1.13 A geographical view of man–environment relationships. *Source:* Pryce (1977).

which is unrealistic for any scale that is less than global. As with the previous model, this one also purports to be value-free.

In presenting this model, Pryce (1977) observed that, ultimately, man and environment cannot be regarded as separate entities. As an alternative, he argued that the systems approach, involving continuous interaction between components, allows for a greater understanding of human ecological relationships.

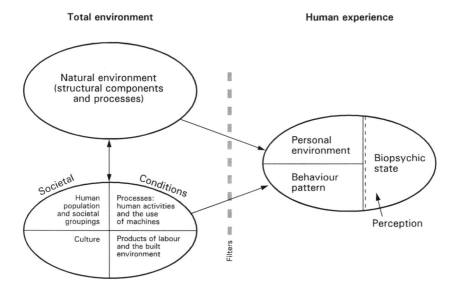

Figure 1.14 The Hong Kong human ecology model – 1. *Source:* Boyden (1979).

29

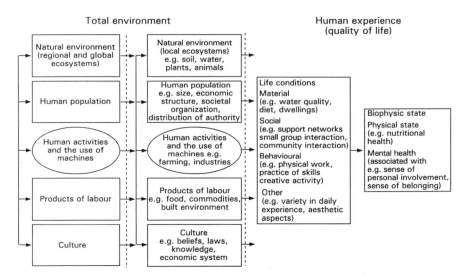

Figure 1.15 The Hong Kong human ecology model – 2. *Source:* Boyden (1979).

Within the paradigm of human ecology, social science perspectives have also been incorporated into more complex conceptual models. One of the best known of these is the model developed by Boyden and colleagues in their study of Hong Kong.

Figures 1.14 and 1.15 represent two versions of the Hong Kong model, proposed for integrative ecological studies of human settlements. The main concern is with the impact of societal conditions on the natural environment and on the quality of human experience (Boyden 1979: 26); it is a reflection of the explicit and intrinsic values for the integrity of ecosystems and the health and wellbeing of people.

This model is exemplary for the efficiency with which it incorporates social, cultural, economic, technological and, especially, psychological factors. The inclusion of "filters" is a noteworthy means for representing cultural and economic differentials in human experience of the total environment.

However, it is unfortunate that this UNESCO-sponsored model excludes, or at least obscures, pertinent political factors. For example, there is little scope for the consideration of government priorities that almost certainly influence ecosystems' integrity as well as the health and wellbeing of people. General human purposes, goals and motives are also conspicuously absent.

Two dynamic models that give greater emphasis to such factors are presented in Figures 1.16 and 1.17. The first model, which was devised by Bennett (1976) to illustrate his theory of ecological transition, emphasizes how natural environment is increasingly used, absorbed, and modified in

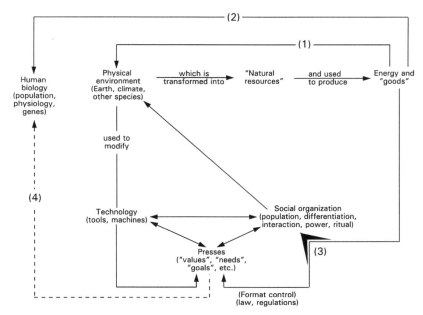

Figure 1.16 A paradigm of human ecology emphasizing the output function. *Source:* Bennett (1976).

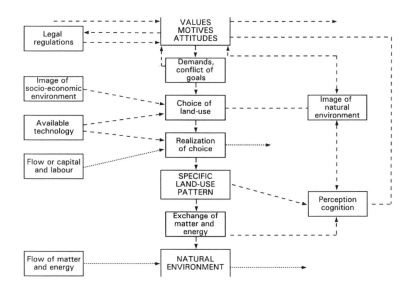

Figure 1.17 A simplified model of the interactions between man and the natural environment on the meso-scale of land-use systems. *Source:* Reidl & Weichhart (1980).

accordance with human productive purposes. In this model, the "presses" are of particular interest: they symbolize the motive force that drives the application of technology and social organization towards further domination of the environment. The presses originate from values, needs and goals, which are considered to be fundamental aspects of political and economic systems.

This model has a distinct and intentional social science orientation. Accordingly, it may be criticized for partially representing the natural environment in an unrealistic and passive light, and as a component that has no impact on human behaviour and towards which human beings need make no adjustment.

The second, by Reidl & Weichhart (1980), is a more elaborate model that emphasizes the role of choice in the processes whereby values, motives and attitudes become manifest in local land use. Unlike the former model, this one does allow for environmental influences upon human behaviour, via human psychological processes. Socio-economic, psychological, technological and legal factors are incorporated as external inputs, whereas political factors are rather obscured. However, "conflicts of goals" may embrace some aspects of local politics, particularly when land-use decisions are made at group and institutional levels.

The notion of levels is emphasized in the model of Clapham & Pestel (1978) shown in Figure 1.18. This model is based on multi-level hierarchical systems theory and is applied as a tool for studying agriculture. Each stratum is connected by information flow including "control information" (from top to bottom) and "process information" (from bottom to top). This model incorporates many of the specific social, economic and political factors that have direct impacts upon agriculture, and thereby upon the natural environment.

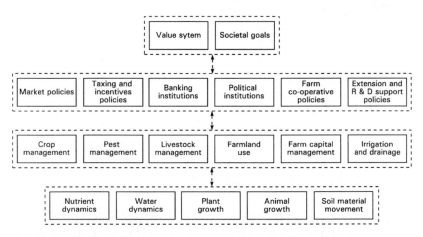

Figure 1.18 Agriculture as a multi-level hierarchical system.
Source: Clapham & Pestel (1978).

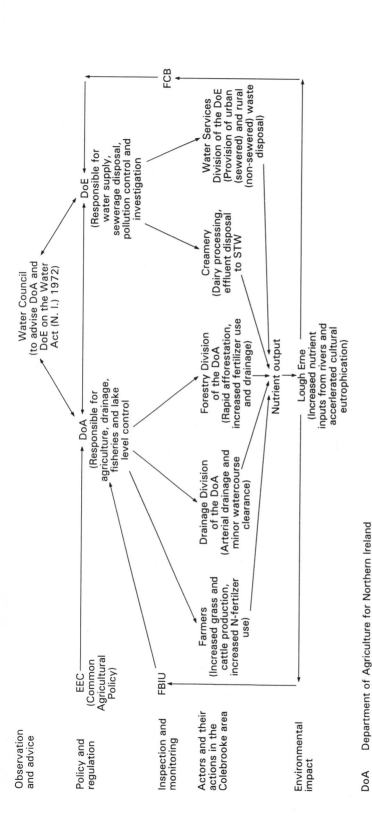

Figure 1.19 Some factors affecting the eutrophication of Lough Erne. *Source:* Phillips-Howard (1985).

DoA   Department of Agriculture for Northern Ireland
DoE   Department of the Environment for Northern Ireland
FBIU   Freshwater Biological Investigation Unit of the DoA
FCB   Fisheries Conservancy Board
STW   Sewerage Treatment Works

Psychological factors are implicitly included in management activities within the individual stratum, and there is no doubt as to the ultimate source of control in the value system and societal goals.

A more specific empirical example of a multi-level hierarchical model is shown in Figure 1.19. It depicts the policies, institutions, immediate actors and their activities that influence the eutrophication of Lough Erne. The emphasis is on the role and impact of policies and institutions regarding eutrophication control. The explicit value is to control the accelerated eutrophication of Lough Erne through alternative policies that involve reduced nutrient losses from agricultural land (Phillips-Howard 1985).

Figure 1.20 is a unique model that incorporates aspects of culture and social organization. Based on the Chinese feng-shui philosophy, this model, translated into landscape planning, has been represented as applied human ecology (Yu 1991). The philosophy is transformed through the logic "source—mechanism—result" into a science of the total human ecosystem in which components including the heavens, the Earth, human beings and their ancestors, and the living environment are linked by the multi-functional flow of qi.

Qi is both the source and the essence of the universe; it may be yin (female) or yang (male) and it accumulates into tangible forms. The mechanisms of atmospheric movement, rotation of the Earth, and the seasons are movements of qi. These, together with the state of qi, which is a function of the planets, landforms, directions, seasons, spiritual (colour) and moral factors, may or may not match harmoniously with each other and the mutual promotion and restraint principles of the five elements, wood, fire, earth, metal and water. As a result of balances among yin and yang and the five elements, the living qi is in harmony and life can flourish. Harmony between man and nature becomes a reality. According to Yu (1991), feng-shui becomes applied human ecology when these principles are incorporated into landscape planning to attain a good (explicitly valued) state of qi and harmony with the elements and with nature as a whole.

1.4 Conclusion

This outline of human ecology was intended to provide an insight into some of the aspects and problems of this research discipline. In so doing, the concept and its historical origins were presented. Questions of methodology included, in particular, the holistic and the integrative approach. Dealing with complexity poses a particular difficulty, and this applies both to the society–nature relationship and to the involvement of the various scientific disciplines that belong to the domain of human ecology. One possibility for coping with complex matters could be to design and apply conceptual models.

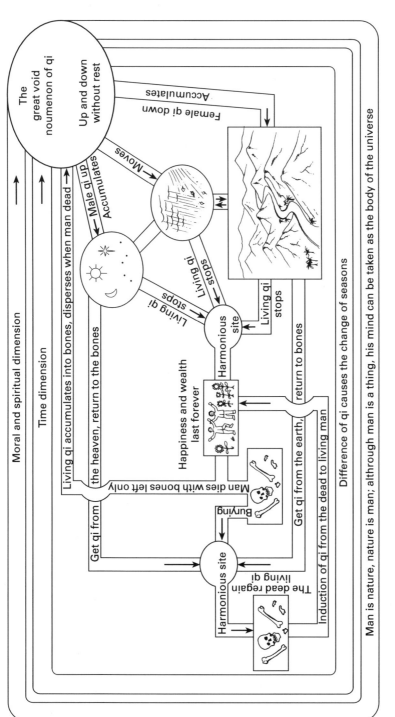

Figure 1.20 The system and flow of qi in feng-shui theory. *Source:* Yu (1991).

Conceptual models were shown to have considerable heuristic value in human ecology. They are particularly useful for integrative, holistic studies and exercises in planning, which transcend unidimensional natural science and social science perspectives. Moreover, even if many of them are not models of reality, together they have their own value as a "checklist" for the design of more appropriate models for human ecology, such that all the variables needed are included. This heuristic function accounts for the apparent heterogeneity of the models featured: some are static, others dynamic, some are mere influence diagrams, others are flow diagrams. The intention in presenting this wide variety was to illustrate the diverse approaches available and building on these to suggest preferable alternatives.

However, viewed individually, there were several shortcomings in many of the models: exclusion of outer-world realities, hidden value judgements, and a failure to reflect a holistic emphasis. The biologically orientated models proved to be unrealistic and inadequate with regard to the role of humans in society and with respect to their natural environment. Many of them appear to be value-free, although this is just about impossible in the ecology of human beings, because the omission of vested interests as a determinant exonerates the resulting behaviour, that is continued exploitation of the environment. An inappropriate emphasis on the biological basis of human ecology and neglect of the "human" aspects make these models largely inconsistent with the holistic concept of ecology as originally defined by Haeckel.

The social-science-inclusive models were generally found to be more appropriate for the scientific advancement of human ecology. However, these models are highly varied and have different levels of aggregation and different emphases with respect to socio-economic factors and processes. Moreover, in some cases the environment's role is insufficiently recognized, with nature cast in an unrealistically passive light. The most appropriate models acknowledge the dynamism of both nature and human activity, but give recognition to human goal-oriented behaviour as the principal source of contemporary ecological change. The task remains to ask the right questions from a holistic perspective, which would include not taking ecological services as given, and to devise and then incorporate appropriate conceptual models in pursuing this objective.

In spite of the brevity of this presentation, it is clear that many of the areas of applied human ecology, now as before, are confronted with a certain deficit in theory. There is still work to be done both here, and where theory and practice meet.[4]

---

4. Some consequences for future thinking and action are drawn in Part Four, which investigates theoretical concepts of nature and features agrarian culture as a human ecological approach to link theory and practice.

CHAPTER 2
Applications for human ecology

As a multidisciplinary science, human ecology has many fields of application. It may even be correct to say that often greater advances have been made in application than in the underlying unifying theory. This chapter constitutes the integrative point where theory and practice meet, and should contribute to a comprehensive theoretical backdrop to the empirical studies that follow in Chapters 5 and 6. Following the conceptual framework of the "Vienna School", the spectrum of topics investigated in human ecology will first be briefly outlined, before one particular area, namely environment and development, is explored. Conceptual models for the application of human ecology to specifically developmental issues are presented, and the question of sustainability is discussed with respect to development (ecodevelopment), agriculture (ecofarming) and other related fields, such as energy use and housing.

2.1 Areas of investigation

Beyond the specific social science and epistemological issues mentioned above, there remains a plethora of additional fields for human ecology. Thus far the most varied, although not yet complete, system is represented by the combined working groups of the IOHE (IOHE 1981; Fig. 2.1). Every given main theme or area of investigation contains several subareas. The working group "habitats", for instance, deals with the "environments" of dwelling, occupation, leisure, and transportation and traffic, i.e. urban development problems. Sociomedical issues come under the main heading "variations of the ecological potency", whose subareas of investigation include the "ecologies" of various age groups and the handicapped, and research into environmentally determined stress. The main area "theory" deals, among other things, with basic concepts, questions of terminology, epistemological aspects, methods and models. Behaviour-orientated subtopics such as ethics, jurisprudence and education fall under the main area "operative aspects". Other subareas such as ecophilosophy, peace and conflict and underdevelopment

MT 1	Main theme "HABITATS"
Hab 0	Principles of gestalting habitats
Hab 1	Residential habitat
Hab 2	Occupational habitat
Hab 3	Regenerational habitat
Hab 4	Circulational habitat
MT 2	Main theme "VARIATIONS OF THE ECOLOGICAL POTENCY"
EcPot	Essence of the ecological potency
PedEc	Pedecology
(PedEc 1)	Pedecology 1
(PedEc 2)	Pedecology 2
(PedEc 3)	Pedecology 3
GamEc	Gamecology
GerEc	Gerontecology
Hand	Human ecological problems of the handicapped
HumE1	The human element in the person-environment-stress setting
MT 3	Main theme "THEORY"
BasConc	Basic concepts
(Term)	Terminology
(MaFem)	The male-female aspect of human being
Epist	Epistemology
M & M	Methods and models

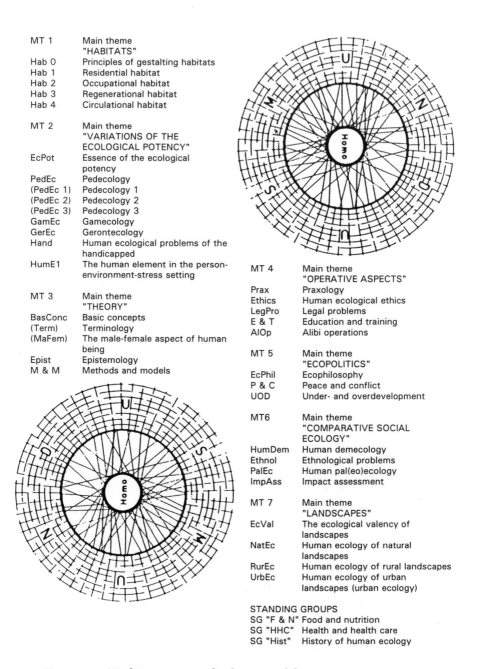

MT 4	Main theme "OPERATIVE ASPECTS"
Prax	Praxology
Ethics	Human ecological ethics
LegPro	Legal problems
E & T	Education and training
AlOp	Alibi operations
MT 5	Main theme "ECOPOLITICS"
EcPhil	Ecophilosophy
P & C	Peace and conflict
UOD	Under- and overdevelopment
MT6	Main theme "COMPARATIVE SOCIAL ECOLOGY"
HumDem	Human demecology
Ethnol	Ethnological problems
PalEc	Human pal(eo)ecology
ImpAss	Impact assessment
MT 7	Main theme "LANDSCAPES"
EcVal	The ecological valency of landscapes
NatEc	Human ecology of natural landscapes
RurEc	Human ecology of rural landscapes
UrbEc	Human ecology of urban landscapes (urban ecology)

STANDING GROUPS
SG "F & N" Food and nutrition
SG "HHC" Health and health care
SG "Hist" History of human ecology

Figure 2.1 Working groups and subgroups of the IOHE. *Source:* IOHE (1981).

and overdevelopment fall under the main category "ecopolitics". "Comparative social ecology" deals, for instance, with questions of social and cultural anthropology and issues related to impact assessment of specific policy measures. Finally, the main theme "landscapes" deals with the human ecologies of natural and rural landscapes, as well as urban ecology. As stated above, this set of categories does not represent a complete classification of all human ecology; nevertheless, it does give a clear overview of the variety and multitude of possible areas of investigation.

To some extent, any attempt to outline the subject matter of a research field will always contain a personal point of view. All organizers of conferences and meetings on human ecology face a decision as to where the limits should be set. Figure 2.1 (similarly Fig. 1.3 in Ch. 1) highlights this inadequacy by situating *Homo* ("man") at the centre of the world (*mundus*): human ecology is responsible for investigating the connections that exist between humans and the remainder of the outside world. Since there are in effect no limits to what could be included as a subtheme, some readers of this book will undoubtedly notice omissions, depending on their individual background.

2.2 Applications to development

The application of the socially orientated human ecological approach to Third World development has been equated with the concept of "ecodevelopment" (Glaeser 1984). This concept was introduced by Maurice Strong, First Executive Director of the United Nations Environment Programme, in 1973. The early perspective of ecodevelopment associated with Sachs (1977) was as an accelerated "style of development", involving attainment of basic needs and human fulfilment within eco-regions, which is compatible with sound management of the environment. This style of development was regarded by Sachs (1980: 113) to involve:

- harmony between consumption patterns, time use and life cycles
- appropriate technologies, ecologically based designs
- low energy profile, promotion of a renewable energy base
- new uses for environmental resources, careful husbandry of resources, recycling
- ecological principles to guide settlement patterns and land uses
- participatory planning and activation of grassroots interests.

According to Redclift (1987), the early perspective of ecodevelopment also bore the benevolently paternalistic imprint common to much planning methodology. The necessity to incorporate social variables has endured in subsequent perspectives of the concept.

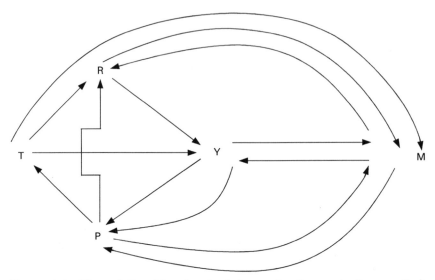

Figure 2.2 The relationships involved in ecodevelopment. *Source:* Sach (1977).

However, the emphasis of ecodevelopment has recently changed with the promotion of the concept of sustainable development (WCED 1987a) and refinements to it.[1] In particular, the integrating concept of "sustainable livelihood security" has orientated ecodevelopment beyond the concern for provision of basic needs towards the priorities and interests of the poor as perceived by themselves (WCED 1987b, Chambers 1988). Moreover, although sustainability (the maintenance or enhancement of resource productivity on a long-term basis) is regarded as an important developmental goal, greater immediate weight is given to livelihoods (adequate stocks or flows of food and cash to meet basic needs) and their security (secure ownership of, or access to, resources and income-generating activities). In the field of ecodevelopment, conceptual models have been used to describe interrelationships, analyze and synthesize problems and assist in the planning of projects; often simultaneously.

Figure 2.2 shows the earliest model of ecodevelopment, which was used by Sachs (1977) to illustrate the relationships involved when the environment (M) is added to the development economist's traditional field of vision, which includes population (P), techniques (T), natural resources (R) and the

---

1. Although there is certainly no contradiction between the concepts of sustainable development and ecodevelopment, a tendency towards conflict between the two terms can be observed. "Sustainability" has become a grossly popular term and may be easily abused. The notion of "ecodevelopment", which precedes the current catch-phrase, may – on the whole – be more correctly descriptive in the context of human ecology (cf. Glaeser 1984: 1-6).

economic product (Y). Action can be directed towards each of these relationships in order to achieve the goals of ecodevelopment. The values associated with this model are those indicated above.

According to Thompson (1977: 282), at the core of ecodevelopment is "political ecology", which relates power relationships, productive forces and forms of organization to physical structures. These relations, including

- the production of goods by utilizing the environment as an economic input,
- the return of organic waste material to the environment as economic output, and
- the role of labour as an essential factor in the production process, which links society with the environment,

are simply illustrated, at a highly aggregated level, in Figure 2.3. Implied values in this model include solidarity with labour and effective utilization of both human and natural resources. The distinctive political economy orientation of this model does, however, seem to render it partial rather than holistic.

At a similar level of aggregation, Figure 2.4 represents two cycles of development with regard to the use of natural resources and human wellbeing.

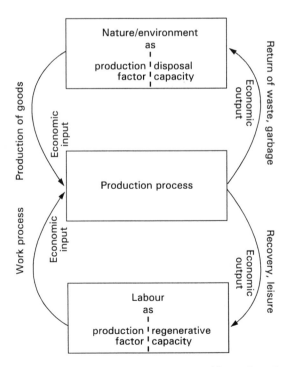

Figure 2.3 Economic processes as viewed by political ecology. *Source:* Phillips-Howard & Glaeser (1983).

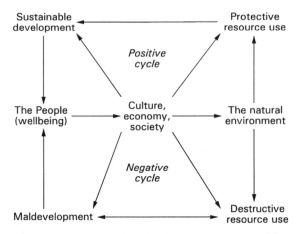

Figure 2.4 Sustainable development versus malde-velopment. *Source:* Phillips-Howard (unpublished).

The implied goal is to emphasize two major development options and to encourage a shift from the negative "maldevelopment" cycle to the positive "sustainable development" cycle. Investment in, support for, and empower-ment of people, plus care for the environment, are explicit values in this model.

At a less aggregated and more specific level, the historical flow model pre-sented in Figure 2.5 describes man–environment change in the tin-mining

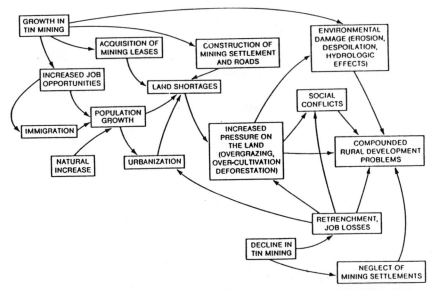

Figure 2.5 Model of man–environment change in the tin-mining areas of the Jos Plateau. *Source:* Adekayi et al. (1990).

42

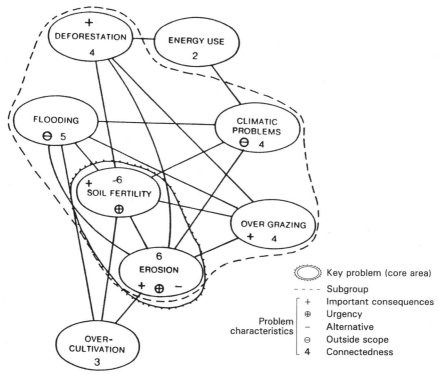

Figure 2.6 An example problem group highlighted. *Source:* Adekayi et al. (1990).

area of the Jos Plateau, Nigeria. It shows how the growth of tin-mining led to increased employment, immigration, and the creation of infrastructure and settlements, but also to land shortage, environmental damage and social conflict (Adekayi et al. 1990).

With the collapse of the tin-mining industry, rural poverty is shown to have been exacerbated by job losses, retrenchment, and neglect of the mining settlements. Although it incorporates specific social, economic, demographic and political factors efficiently, this model can be criticized for an apparent neglect of external relationships, although they are to some extent reflected in the growth and decline of the tin-mining industry. The same values as for the previous model are evident here, but they are implicit rather than explicit (Adekayi et al. 1990).

A recent example of a problem-orientated model, which is also used in planning, is the adaptation and use of the strategic choice approach (Friend & Hickling 1987) to human ecological research in the Jos Plateau tin-mining region (Adekayi et al. 1990). The procedure involves:

- listing and then grouping problems
- establishing linkages within groups and highlighting certain problems, and

43

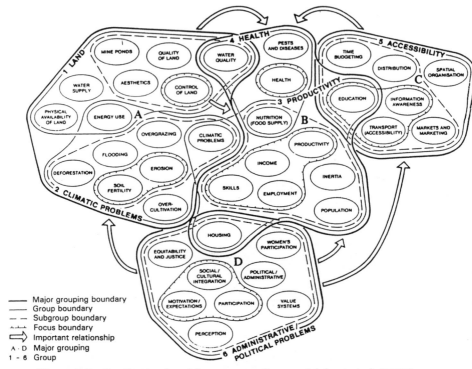

Figure 2.7 Synthesis of problem groups. *Source:* Adekayi et al. (1990).

• identifying relationships between problem groups as a basis for synthesizing them into wholes.

Figure 2.6 illustrates the preliminary stages of the procedure, whereas Figure 2.7 shows how the problem groups are synthesized. The approach explicitly incorporates the planners' understanding and value judgements in the identification of problems and linkages, in the highlighting exercise and in the synthesis of problem groups. In the case study the values were those of highly educated, urban-based, Nigerian elite males. These were reflected, for example, in the exclusion of "women's issues" by one working group and its modification to "women's participation" by another.

The most useful feature of this approach is that it enables planners to give priority to problems according to their characteristics, e.g. urgency, importance of their consequences, alternatives by which they may be tackled, and connectivity, so that they may plan effective interventions. This approach offers considerable scope for applied human ecological studies, not least because of its synthetic aspect. But, since the outcomes closely reflect the specific interests and values of the participants, a broad multidisciplinary mix is needed to avoid partiality and bias. However, for maximum benefit to be derived from this approach, the participation of local communities is also

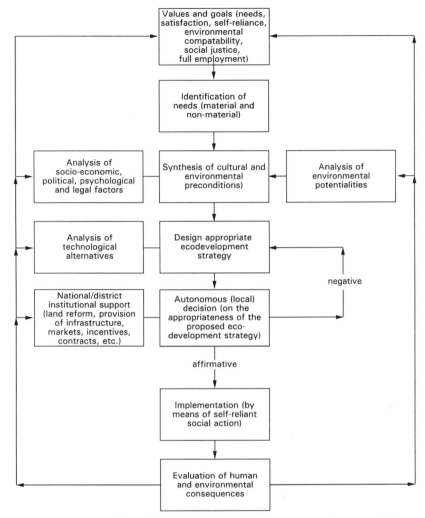

Figure 2.8 A model of the ecodevelopment process – 1. *Source:* Phillips-Howard & Glaeser (1983).

needed so that their priorities, knowledge and values may also be taken into account.

A conceptual model that describes the process of ecodevelopment in a straightforward and schematic way, and is also a useful planning guide, is shown in Figure 2.8. In common with the multi-level hierarchical model (Fig. 1.18) presented by Clapham & Pestel (1978), this one starts at the top with values and goals, but then differs in that control is largely vested in the local communities. This model has been explained in detail elsewhere with reference to a case study from Tanzania (Phillips-Howard & Glaeser 1983).

45

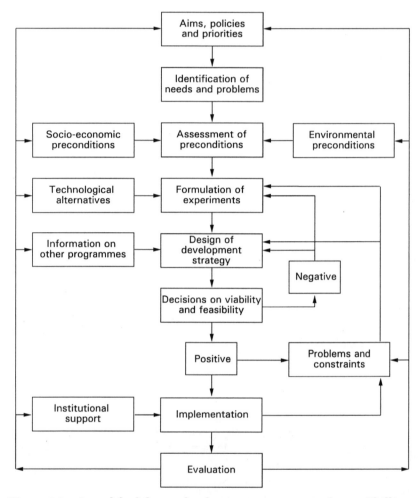

Figure 2.9 A model of the ecodevelopment process – 2. *Source:* Phillips-Howard (1989).

The model has, however, recently been modified for use in finding viable solutions to human ecological problems on the Jos Plateau, Nigeria (Phillips-Howard 1989). The refined and more iterative version (Fig. 2.9) incorporates replanning in response to the problems and constraints that arise at the implementation stage, and gives greater emphasis to community participation in the planning process.

Whereas Figure 2.8 described a project in which the planners generated "packages of ecological production methods" for introduction through pilot schemes, Figure 2.9 was introduced as a guide for a programme in which "baskets of choices" are generated based largely on local perceptions and priorities.

Figure 2.10a is a highly localized and specific model to illustrate rice fields as agro-ecosystems. They are essentially seen as ecological systems transformed by human action to produce food and fibre (Conway 1987). Despite the apparent biological orientation of this model (compare with Newbould's model, Fig. 1.6), it is actually an efficiently designed social-science–inclusive one, since it includes human activity within a socio-economic boundary, although with minimum elaboration. Moreover, it is acknowledged that the basic ecological processes of the system are overlaid and regulated by the agricultural processes of cultivation, subsidy, control, harvesting and marketing, and that the system is dominated by human goals and the consequences of social and economic co-operation and competition.

Having defined agro-ecosystems to include socio-economic components, Conway (1987) envisions a hierarchy of such systems, as shown in Figure 2.10b.

The values explicitly associated with the agro-ecosystems model are social value (defined in terms of the amount of goods and services produced, their relationship to human needs or happiness, and their allocation among the human population) and some derived measurable properties such as productivity, stability, sustainability and equitability – all of which can be used normatively for evaluation purposes (Conway 1987).

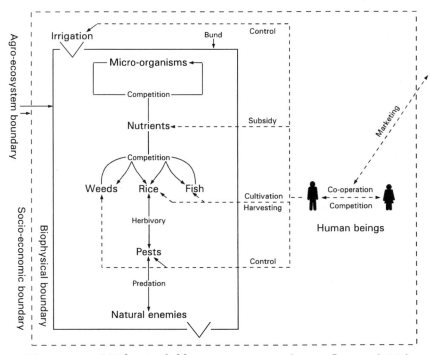

Figure 2.10 (a) The rice fields as an ecosystem. *Source:* Conway (1987).

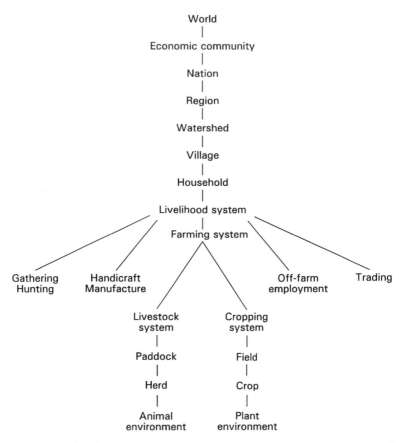

Figure 2.10   (b) The hierarchy of agro-ecosystems. *Source:* Conway (1987).

Finally, two of the most significant conceptual models concerned with ecodevelopment are shown in Figure 2.11a,b. The first illustrates the argument that, if sustainable livelihood security is to be attained, then "sustainable livelihood thinking" is required among development professionals. As conceived by Chambers (1988), sustainable livelihood thinking (SLT) combines concerns for environment, development and livelihoods, and starts with the needs and priorities of the poor. This integration enables causal connections to be made among these elements; connections that have been largely overlooked by adherents to "environment thinking", "development thinking" and "livelihood thinking". It thereby helps to set an agenda for future training, research and action in ecodevelopment that would focus on these connections.

Figure 2.11b specifies linkages neglected by professionals who lack SLT. These linkages may be critical to resource-poor farmers (Chambers 1988).

	FT	DT	LT		SLT
The people concerned	Traditional biologists and conservationists	Traditional economists and "developers"	The very poor	The poor	New professionals
Primary focus	The environment	Production	Livelihood survival	Livelihood security	Achieving adequate, secure and sustainable livelihoods
Major criteria in decision-making and evaluation	Conservation of resources Maintenance of diversity	Ecomic growth Productivity and economic returns	Immediate satisfacton of basic needs	Basic needs plus security	Sustainable gains by the very poor Livelihood security for all
Time horizon Value place on the future	Long Higher than present	Medium Lower than present	Short Lower than by the poor	Short and long Higher than by the very poor	Moving from short and low (survival) to long and high (sustainability)
Normal structure of thinking { ends { means	-ve ↗E↘ -ve D◄·······L	+ve ↗D↘ +ve E◄·······L	+ve ↗L↘ +ve D·······►E	+ve ↗SL↘ +ve D◄——►E +ve

The continuous arrows represent causal connections and directions emphasized in the way of thinking. The dotted arrows represent connections that are recognized but not stressed. The heavy arrow under SLT is an intervention.

E   Environment, including natural resources

D   Development

L   Livelihoods

SL   Sustainable livelihoods

Figure 2.11 (a) Modes of thinking compared. *Source:* Chambers (1988).

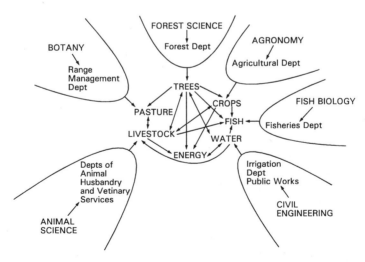

Gaps neglected by normal professionalism are represented by most of the lines in the centre, which often represent linkages critical to resource-poor farmers.

Figure 2.11 (b) Professions, departments, interactions and gaps. *Source:* Chambers (1988).

Earlier perspectives of ecodevelopment allegedly attempted to "steal or borrow some sociological content, either through social planning norms or through referring to basic needs and self-reliance" (Redclift 1987). Sachs' model (Fig. 2.2) was actually built by adding environment (M) to the development economist's field of vision. Hence, if any stealing or borrowing occurred in this case it was from natural science to social science and not vice versa. Nevertheless, Chambers' (1988) perspective is acknowledged here as a real advance because of the explicit value it attaches to the poor and its recognition that they understand their own circumstances and know very well how they can be improved. As Chambers (1988) indicates, the appropriate policy strategy implied by this perspective is to give priority to livelihood improvement in the short term so as to create the conditions for sustainable livelihood-intensive use of the environment over the long term.

2.3 Sustainable development

Ecodevelopment as applied human ecology

In the following, the theoretical structure of human ecology will be applied to concrete economic and ecological development problems. Most developing countries have gone through a long phase of economic and ecological exploitation, not only during colonial times, but also after gaining political independence. The export of basic materials and food to the industrialized countries is coupled with the importation of manufactured goods produced by these countries in a process in which the exchange relations, the so-called terms of trade are, with few exceptions, very unfavourable for the developing countries.

In contrast, the policy of ecodevelopment (Glaeser 1984) or sustainable development is a co-operative approach that also includes "co-operation" with nature and the environment. In so doing, ecodevelopment, which was first propagated and supported by the United Nations Environment Programme (UNEP) in the 1970s, is understood as another type of strategy for socio-economic development that is constructed on elements of self-reliance and need orientation (including participation), while giving consideration to environmental compatibility. The goal is income redistribution in favour of the most disadvantaged regions of the Earth, whereby importance is attached to production based on long-term sustainability of the environment and conservation of natural resources. These elements are embedded in the sectors of economy, society and ecology within the human ecological or politico-ecological concept (Table 2.1).

Self-reliance means a certain degree of autonomy, which is not to say that it is comparable to the quest for autarky. Although a partial dissociation from

Table 2.1 Political ecology of the developing countries.

Political ecology	Ecodevelopment	Ecofarming
Economy	Self-reliance	Yield
Society and culture	Need orientation	Mixed cultivation
Ecology	Environmental compatibility	Erosion control and soil fertility

the world market can produce temporary beneficial results for the development of an internal market, this cannot be understood as constituting a goal
in itself. A necessary condition is still the use of local human and natural
potential and resources. Emphasis must be placed on the two-sidedness of
the interaction context, human–human on the one hand, and human–nature
on the other.

In need orientation the concentration and activity is centred on supporting, above all, the most impoverished groups of inhabitants with the necessary means for satisfying their needs, and is specifically opposed to assumed
efficacy of the so-called "trickle-down" effect, the gradual extension of the
benefits of economic development downwards to the most needy population
strata. Here it is important to note that the means of need satisfaction – i.e.
food, clothing, housing, medical care and education – be provided during the
course of the individual work process. Alongside "material" satisfaction in
the form of money or subsistence income, attention must be given to "social"
satisfaction within the context of the work process. This goal can be
achieved, for example, through participation of the affected persons in measures and projects associated with developmental aid.

Giving consideration to environmental compatibility is understood to
mean the preservation of the ecological basis needed for the economic process. Within the context of agriculture, which is now as before the most
important production sector, this includes prevention of erosion and maintaining soil fertility. Soil, as the most important agricultural resource, must
not be overworked or overexploited. Rather, the system of agriculture and its
immanent natural processes must be dealt with as an agro-ecosystem.

Agriculture as an agro-ecosystem

Ecologically appropriate production methods, or ecofarming (Rottach 1988),
constitute the agrotechnical application of ecodevelopment. The principles
of ecofarming can be summarized under the following three headings (Egger
1979: 243):
- ordered productive diversity
- economic cycles
- biological erosion control.

51

Table 2.2 Alternative farming methods.

Seed–fertilizer technology	Ecofarming
Productive simplification of the system	Productive, guided system diversity
Specialization	Product diversity
Separation of tree, field, fodder cultivation, animal husbandry, and speciality crop cultivation	Integration of tree, field, fodder cultivation, animal husbandry, and speciality crop cultivation
Linear matter and energy throughput	Self-sustaining matter and energy cycles
Fertility through artificial fertilizers and biocides	Fertility through high biomass turnover
High inputs	Low inputs
High yield	Medium yield
Low stability	High stability
Intensive mechanical processing	Moderate mechanical processing
Mechanical erosion control	Biological erosion control
Fences	Hedgerows
Low-resistance, high-yield varieties	High-resistance, medium-yield varieties
Monoculture	Mixed culture
Elimination of weeds	Tolerance of weeds
Low energy efficiency	High energy efficiency

Source: after Egger (1979: 241 f.).

These principles aid ecofarming and help to maintain or increase soil fertility, which is based on soil quality, water supply and biological–ecological potential. A comparison of ecological and conventional agriculture (Table 2.2) reveals that the application of such principles can by no means be taken for granted. Seed–fertilizer technology, which was also the basis of the "green revolution" in developing countries, is based on the desire for short-term maximization of yield and profit; in many cases, the result is that the soil, agricultural capital *par excellence*, is ravaged. Ecofarming relies to a great extent on the natural properties and strengths of the ecosystem, whereas seed–fertilizer technology is forced to resort to incomparably higher anthropogenic applications of energy. In addition, the environment has been contaminated by the excessive use of agrochemicals. Finally, food quality has deteriorated, be it indirectly, through the plant—animal—human chain, or directly, through the use of pharmaceutical preparations and medicines.

Consequences for food quality, environmental pollution and energy use

It may have become apparent that the principles and measures of eco-development apply not only to the developing, but also to the industrialized countries. The reason is that not only "underdevelopment" but also certain forms of "overdevelopment" produce deleterious effects on humans and nature. They represent two aspects of economic and ecological maldevelopment. Several examples of this will be mentioned below.

FOOD QUALITY

Consumers in industrialized countries have been becoming increasingly aware in recent years of the fact that a large portion of fruits and vegetables offered for sale leave much to be desired in freshness and taste, whereas meat has often not been hung and contains too much water. The food industry has concentrated on superficial criteria such as appearance, eat-by dates, and transportability. Consumers as well as producers adapt; taste and habits change. The result has been a learning effect in favour of new, reduced quality expectations.

Unfortunately, food quality data are extremely difficult to come by. This is because for methodological – perhaps also political – reasons, unified standards for quality have not yet been established. One possible solution to the problem would be to limit analysis to individual quality components and substances contained in products. In this way, for example, it was possible, using a study of apples, to determine that yield maximization is not compatible with needs for optimum quality. The findings of Stoll in 1969 indicate that a medium increase in yield quality criteria such as fruit flesh colour, peel colour, taste, perishability and texture could be optimized by doubling nitrate use. Such a finding would not be difficult to achieve with the ecofarming method. Higher applications of nitrate in the study would negatively influence quality, however, whereas yields could also be increased by a fourfold application of nitrate.

ENVIRONMENTAL QUALITY

Various production methods produce different effects on economy and ecology, not only on the individual farm, but beyond its boundaries as well. These are referred to as "external effects". Positive external effects can be seen in landscape conservation, for example, and the recreational effect this has, especially in areas not far from the city. It is fairly certain that the use of such nearby recreational areas contributes, among other things, to a reduction in social medical costs. Negative external effects are karst development, salting and erosion of the soil. Over-use results in humus depletion and a decrease in soil fertility. The use of chemical fertilizers in industrially managed chemotechnical agriculture has led, in many cases, to nitrate washout and eutrophication, i.e. overfertilization, and with it reduction in the oxygen content of water supplies (Conrad 1990). The sprayed biocides often contaminate the air, destroy micro-organisms in the soil and destroy beneficial insects that would otherwise help to eliminate pests. Here, the methods of ecofarming offer the advantage that they lessen damage to the environment through decreased use of chemicals and the conscious maintenance of the ecosystem's species diversity. An exact quantitative, even comparative, evaluation of environmental pollution is very difficult to provide, however, since effect mechanisms and secondary and tertiary effects are often not known.

ENERGY USE

Corn yields in the USA more than doubled with respect to field size between 1945 and 1970, while nitrate fertilizer use has increased 16 times. Biocide use soared from 0 to 55000 kcal per hectare. Mechanical equipment, fuel consumption and nitrate fertilizing consume the most energy, i.e. roughly three-quarters of total energy consumption. The ratio of energy yield (in the form of food) to energy consumption (excluding solar energy) worsened by about a quarter, from 3.7 in 1945 to 2.8 in 1970 (Pimentel et al. 1973).

The energy ratio continues to worsen substantially if the refining industry and storage and processing are also taken into consideration. The USA system of food production increased its total energy use from planting to consumption between 1940 and 1970 more than threefold. Since, on the other hand, food consumption remained constant with respect to population growth, the ratio of consumed food energy and gross energy input in food production fell from about 1:5 to about 1:10, i.e. by one-half (Steinhart & Steinhart 1974).

The fact that ecofarming also represents an alternative with respect to energy conservation is revealed in a comparative study carried out by Lockeretz and his colleagues in the corn belt of the USA. Equal or only slightly smaller yields in ecologically orientated corn production were achieved with the help of an expenditure of only about one-third as much energy as is used on a comparable, conventionally managed farm (Lockeretz et al. 1975). Similar results were reached in comparative studies conducted in the Federal Republic of Germany and in the Netherlands (Ronnenberg 1973).

The relative waste of energy in chemotechnical agriculture becomes even clearer in developing countries, where substantially less energy is used. The extent to which the introduction of seed–fertilizer technology has changed conditions, however, can be seen in the Chinese example. Although vegetable and rice cultivation in Hong Kong still revealed an energy ratio (based on the relation of energy yield to energy application) of 24.4 in the 1930s, this sank to 1.3 by 1971, whereas intensive cultivation only reached 0.13 (Newcombe 1975).

In arranging the various previously ascertained energy rates – although they could not always be compared – one is able to differentiate between three food systems (Leach 1976):

- Ranging between energy rates of 0.01 and 0.05, fisheries fared worst, with fish-meal processing largely to blame.
- In the middle we find agriculture in the industrialized countries, which, according to the degree of industrialization, ranged from 0.1 to 4.0.
- The best energy use is achieved by traditional cultivation methods used

in developing countries, namely, values between 5.0 and 70.0.

Now, this finding does not mean that traditional production methods found in the developing countries should be introduced everywhere. Because energy use is absolutely very low, high utilization rates are more easily attained, especially since solar energy is not included as a constant in the equation. Nevertheless, a degree of over- or maldevelopment still seems to occur. One politically, economically and ecologically acceptable consequence would be to take the strategy recommendations of ecodevelopment seriously and apply them to the area of ecologically orientated agricultural techniques more strongly than has been done before. This applies to the industrialized as well as to the developing countries, although there are, of course, differences due to exceptional climatic-ecological as well as sociocultural and politico-economic circumstances.[2]

Sustainable agricultural policy

The twofold concept of nature utilization through human labour – both of which are factors of production – can help to bridge the gap from natural and social science to agriculture. Werner Bätzing (Bätzing 1988) speaks of production and reproduction (in a non-Marxist sense): production of foodstuffs necessitates the reproduction of the agro-ecosystem, with the help of regenerative and preservative labour. Neither production nor reproduction can be seen in isolation. Originally, virgin land ("nature") had to be developed and cultivated ("cultured") by humans before it was suited to agriculture or cattle-grazing. This task was performed by human labour. Later, the cultivable land that results from this process, the agro-ecosystem, must be cared for and regenerated – through tilling the soil or compensating for nutrient losses by fertilization – if it is not to become depleted.

The following tentative formula applies here: the more reproductive labour is applied, the better the agro-ecosystem functions. The reverse is also true: the less such labour is invested, the greater is the danger of environmental destruction. The anthropogenic alpine pasture ecosystem, for example, would soon collapse without reproductive labour, as would the associated alpine pastoral economy, without the constant care that is provided by pasture herdsmen (Bätzing 1985).

Just what, and in which combination, humans produce in any given agro-ecosystem is to a certain extent determined by nature, i.e. by locational factors. Agricultural production is also culturally determined, however, for example by nutritional customs, labour organization and techniques, tradition and even religious taboos. Nature does not prescribe – to assume so

---

2. As an example of the attempt to reconcile the issues of environment and development politically and economically, Chapter 5 is devoted to the People's Republic of China.

would be a "naturalistic fallacy" (cf. §3.2) – but does indeed react to inappropriate behaviour.

In the context of holistic human ecology sketched in Chapter 1, we refer to the productive interaction between humans and nature in rural areas as agriculture in the sense of agrarian culture (for details, see Ch. 7: Agrarian culture between conceptual reconstruction and empirics). Agrarian culture encompasses:

- food production adapted to local conditions
- cultivation (latin: *colere, cultura*) of the basis of production
- nutritional customs and preferences adapted to the given area
- the inhabitants living together in a community
- division of labour in the family and the village
- a village agrarian constitution governing rights of property, use and inheritance;
- celebrations and rites, especially those associated with birth, marriage and death.

The unity of productive and reproductive labour, which is self-evident in agrarian cultures, becomes lost in modern agro-industry. Maintenance of the cultivated landscape and species and biotope preservation are becoming completely separated in terms of both agrarian and environmental policy from the production of food, an example of partial – as opposed to holistic – thinking and action.

If, from the political point of view, one wishes to establish guidelines for action, either for the maintenance or the restoration of a holistic, i.e. productive and environmentally benign system of agriculture, then it will be necessary to develop strategies for an agriculturally and environmentally sustainable policy that reintegrates into the system of production that type of labour that preserves nature and the traditional landscape or, in the words of environmental economics and from a commercial point of view, internalizes its own social costs.

Sustainable housing

A relatively recent departure is the application of the human ecology and ecodevelopment approach to other policy fields. Habitat is one such field, where the target is no longer the basic need for food, but the basic need for shelter prevalent among rural populations. The three criteria of ecodevelopment are identified here as house-related problems and desires, such as shelter against environmental forces, space and comfort (sociocultural needs); locally available building materials and construction know-how (self-reliance); and recycling of organic matter via composting or the production of biogas energy (environmental compatibility). This approach considers house and household not only as part of a social system, but also as part of a human–ecological system. Such a system is ideally depicted as a cyclic flow of matter and energy produced to a large extent on a self-reliant basis. It is determined by the needs of the household members, their sociocultural values and their economic strength. (For an empirical study on "ecohousing", see Glaeser 1995).

2.4 Conclusion

There is a multitude of possibilities for applying human ecology, only a few of which have been outlined here. Although different types of classification would certainly be feasible, the one presented above is perhaps the most systematic and, if not entirely comprehensive, does cover a wide range. The focus of this book concerns environmental issues as related to development and agriculture, but this does not imply that other questions are not of equal importance. For example, the following issues are equally deserving of investigation within this context: population pressure, Third World debt, carrying capacity models, ecosystem resilience, "deep ecology", Eastern perspectives and ecological economics.

In the context of Third World development, ecodevelopment models, like the conceptual models presented in Chapter 1, also vary greatly with respect to level of aggregation, purpose (which ranges from description, through analysis and synthesis of problems, to use as a planning tool) and emphasis. The emphasis of the models partly reflects the progress of ideas from the "top-down" provision of basic needs towards the "bottom-up" realization of sustainable livelihood security with greater participation by the target groups. It is difficult to portray the links between the agro-ecological micro-level and the socio-economic input and control mechanisms at the meso-level, which are in turn influenced by macro-level social values and national policies. It is these complex interlinkages, however, which define the subject matter of human ecology *per definitionem*.

In recent years, but specifically during and after the UNCED conference in 1992, sustainability has become the focus of political attention. The concept of ecodevelopment as applied human ecology is just one variable, but in itself an extremely complex issue. Food policy alone, for example, involves crop-production patterns, pollution considerations, energy use and consumer-orientated values. The ecodevelopment approach, however, can, in principle, also be applied to other policy fields, for example habitat systems.

PART TWO
Ethical–political dimensions

CHAPTER 3
Environmental ethics: possibilities and limits

Environmental ethics, it seems, cannot contribute all that much to a reduction in environmental pollution. If this is indeed the case, why is there such frequent and detailed discussion on what the basis for these ethics should be? Time and again in popular literature and Sunday speeches, ethics is cited as a means to influence the behaviour of individuals, and, on a larger scale, the moral will of societies, such that their political classes treat nature properly, that is with concern for preservation.

Since it is fairly obvious that moral suasions and appeals have little consequence on the individual level, let alone on the national or global level, we are led to ask what exactly environmental ethics are and, further, what are they good for? What do they comprise and how do they function? Are our expectations regarding the effectiveness of ethics perhaps too high? This chapter attempts to provide an answer to the above questions, specifically investigating the role of environmental ethics in the conception and implementation of environmental policy. In order to do so, it is first necessary to delve into the concept of ethics itself and deal with some of the fundamental contradictions to be found there. Rather than attempt to encompass the wealth of literature already engendered by research on ecological ethics and its many facets, the discussion here will deal only with central elements and adhere as closely as possible to the human ecological tradition.

3.1 Ethics between knowledge and action

In addition to its theoretical and empirical tasks, human ecology also encompasses normative aspects. These proceed from the assumption that human ecology as a theory of social action should also contribute to solving environmental problems. Thus the orientation towards action in the theoretical analysis is supplemented by the orientation towards action in the normative approach: environmental ethics. Environmental norms play an important role quantitatively in setting standards or threshold levels, and qualitatively in providing criteria for environmental quality standards. However, when environmental standards of any kind are set, the impression is often given that these are derived directly from the findings of scientific research. This is an epistemological error, since norms are established *ex definitione*. In fact, the establishing of ethical values is much more closely associated with conditions related to science, a process that is often not made explicitly clear.

Political action, that is the implementation of measures, is the final manifestation of ethical norms for action. Here, legal and economic instruments, in the form of legislation and guidelines in the context of the given economic system, have precedence.

Ethics seeks an answer to the question: What ought we do? Its object is thus "right" action. Human ecological ethics is therefore a partial moral philosophy that concerns itself with the right environmental behaviour of humans. Theoretical human ecology provides the basis for this philosophy. Environmental ethics inspired by human ecology lean primarily in the direction of the material value approach as opposed to, for example, Kant's moral ethics (cf. Reichardt 1976, Schöndorfer 1976).

Section 3.2 asks whether perhaps an ethical system that emphasizes formal directives for action instead of material values would be more consistent in itself, or whether it would be better to derive ethical environmental norms from social ethics rather than from individual ethics. But we must also ask whether a system of environmental ethics makes any sense at all. One purpose is that subjective behaviour is changed to such an extent that this results in the mitigation of environmental damage. However, previous experience has shown that ethics as an instrument of environmental policy has not been very effective. The politico-administrative enforcement of norms promises to have greater impact. The range of instruments extends from decrees and prohibitions by the legislative process to fiscal policy incentives through subsidies or taxes. Political realization with the aid of legal and economic measures means that economy and law must be brought into harmony with ecology – at times against the vested interests of groups.

3.2 Ethics between human ecology and philosophical tradition

Normative actions and ethics

Perceived from the point of view of social science, human ecology, as a science that includes the study of human behaviour, is also concerned with theories of action. The following perspectives can be differentiated:

61

- the role of action in scientific analysis and empirical study (theory)
- the role of action in the establishment of norms (ethics)
- the role of action in practice and implementation (policy).

The term "human ecological ethics" has two meanings: "On the one hand, it involves ethical problems, the solutions to which can be found in the specialized knowledge of human ecological disciplines. On the other hand, such a concept formulation results from the axiological basis of the science of human ecology itself" (Reichardt 1976: 529). Since all ethics should be applicable to ecological issues or to environmental behaviour, the following questions arise:

- Which ethical view is to be taken as the basis for the ethics of human ecology or environmental ethics?
- What makes human ecological ethics distinct from "general" ethics?

The systematic position of ethics is determined on the basis of the following three questions posed by Kant: "What can I know?" "What ought I do?" "What may I hope?" (Kant 1781: 804 f.; or 1787: 832 f.). The first question refers to epistemology, the second to ethics as the so-called "practical" philosophy, and the third to happiness or theology. *Tà ethikà* – in Greek that which concerns morality or character – refers to "practice" in the sense of human action. Ethics or moral philosophy as the "practical" part of philosophy is thus the science that has moral will and human action as its subject matter and which investigates their underlying conditions. The ethics of human ecology, therefore, is that part of moral philosophy that deals with "right" human actions in terms of the environment.

Ever since Aristotle established ethics as a special discipline of philosophy, the historical course of philosophy has been marked by a variety of successive and, in part, contradictory attempts to provide a logical basis for moral philosophy, from which a set of moral principles may be derived. Contemporary discussion was most profoundly influenced by the formalistic versus material derivation of principles debate in ethics. Although formalism posits a general axiom or set of axioms that must be applied according to certain rules, non-formalistic (material) ethical systems hypothesize or develop sets (as a rule, limited ones) of specific maxims or moral values (value theory) that translate into action on a case-by-case basis.

Value theory and human ecology

To the extent that its contours can be recognized, human ecologically inspired environmental ethics appears to lean more towards the material value approach. Although human ecology cannot and should not, any more so than any other science, make value determinations on its own, it can help to define prerequisites and consequences clearly (Reichardt & Schöndorfer 1977: 132), in service of an ethics of human ecology.

A human ecological value theory of the kind presented paradigmatically by Reichardt in his "Prolegomena" (1976: 530 f.) consists of two elements: the attribution of value by a subject and the consequences of his/her action. Three natural principles are interjected once a set of values has been agreed upon: survival or conservation, wellbeing or avoidance of suffering, development of potential. Finally, two other principles derived from the ecosystem are added: halting irreversible interventions into nature and maximizing species diversification. All five principles taken together, then, constitute the essential maxims of a human ecological value theory, which a human subject acting in an ethically right way must observe.

Here we are confronted with the critical question concerning the basis for their justification (*Grund ihrer Möglichkeit*) which is subdivided below:
- How do value attributions gain intersubjective validity?
- What are the criteria for derivation of these principles?
- How do ethical maxims become imperatives and how is this justified?

Because the derivation of rules for action has neither been completely substantiated, nor are its origins clear, contradictory demands (dilemmas) arise from the ethical maxims, as Reichardt has also pointed out. There are three ways to resolve the antinomies that arise in the area of action and application:
- by positing a "highest" (i.e. an absolute) good
- through the retroactive introduction of formal principles in value theory
- through a casuistry of plausible arguments for case-by-case pragmatic rules for action.

Logically, the first of these solutions cannot be correct, since a material value theory presupposes the existence of some highest value. Although formalistic solutions represent an independent approach to ethics that can be regarded as a real alternative to material value theory, only the pragmatic solution, in so far as it also proceeds from intrinsic values, can be called upon to supplement and thereby rescue human ecological value theory.

Eudaemonistic value theory

One approach of human ecological ethics that was developed in the USA is, to a large degree, casuistic. Based upon studies of global limits to growth, several members of the Massachusetts Institute of Technology (MIT) have drawn conclusions in ethics that would make "quality of life" the highest value. Thus, values and maxims for action were not really separated here. Randers & Meadows (1971) distinguish between short- and long-term maxims, where the decisive criterion is that ethics also gives consideration to temporality. It makes a difference, namely, whether we conduct our activities within the limited horizons of the present or whether we also take into consideration the consequences of our actions for future generations. The authors imagine cost–benefit analyses that encompass the time horizon of the next 100–200 years. Normally such systems aim only at maximum benefit for the present. In contrast to previously known concepts, however, according to Randers & Meadows, benefits are to be set not only against present, but also against future costs. This implies limiting side-effects, which means that the short-term goal of maximizing benefits can be pursued only in so far as this function does not jeopardize the economic and social options of future generations.

The maxims for action are based – and it is here that Forrester (1971c) introduces an additional criterion – upon specific values anchored in society. He claims that religion and ethics should act as the guardians of these values. It must be borne in mind, of course, that on Forrester's view the system of socially accepted goals and values has disintegrated because of internal contradictions, in particular the above-mentioned temporal conflict between present and future, and the question of action for the short or for the long term. According to Forrester, values are a product of the time in which they arise; whenever they are at variance with reality, they must be changed. This is especially true for the ethical foundations of Christianity, the religion of exponential growth. Egocentric ethics of growth must give way to ethical values that encompass the human environment. Forrester concludes that ethics must be made compatible with the dynamic realities of the social system.

The aim is to achieve a "golden age" of balance between humanity and nature, of harmony with the ecosystem of the planet Earth (Randers & Meadows 1971). The highest value of this social Utopian concept would thus be to optimize quality of life for the individual. Forrester describes what he means as follows:

> Raising the quality of life means releasing stress and pressures, reducing crowding, reducing pollution, alleviating hunger, and treating ill-health. . . . To try to raise the quality of life without intentionally creating compensating pressures to prevent a rise in population density will be self-defeating. (Forrester 1971b: 218)

Accordingly, quality of life is to be understood as a set of generally recognized human social needs and values, the satisfaction of which depends upon limiting population density.

The problem with the pragmatic MIT approach becomes evident. The introduction of historical variables in the behavioural system tends to take some of the starch out of the claim of material values to absoluteness; with this, however, the danger arises that ethical norms can be adapted affirmatively to unfavourable realities as well. Therefore, this approach does not provide a way out of human ecology's ethical value dilemma.

This problem is readily apparent in the relatively vague concept of quality of life, which has appeared as the most recent form of eudaemonism. Eudae-monism is defined as that type of material value ethics according to which the morality of human actions is determined on the basis of their intention and ability to produce *eudaimonia*, or happiness. Because of the many ways in which happiness can be defined, eudaemonism assumes a variety of forms extending from Epicurian hedonism to the social eudaemonic concept of social welfare. Quantitative growth, just as does qualitative melioration, con-tributes to the socially organized attainment of happiness, for example the greatest possible happiness for the greatest number (Hutcheson 1694–1746). Both quantitative growth and qualitative melioration in representing the common good embody a social eudaemonistic approach.

Thus, it appears that only a formalistic ethical system, which replaces absolute intrinsic values with absolute criteria, will have long-term rele-vance, because it can withstand changes in subjective values without itself degenerating into arbitrariness or meaninglessness.

Formal ethics

What distinguishes formalistic ethics from the principle of eudaemonism is the fact that the latter is based upon empirical principles, the former upon general rules. This distinction goes back to Immanuel Kant, who attacked eudaemonistic value ethics with a ferocity bordering upon sheer polemics, and with the precision and methodology proper to mathematical science (Kant 1788: 122; 1993: 72) developed pure ethics as a set of autonomously willed, formal, *a priori*, absolute propositions. According to Kant, "all prac-tical principles which presuppose an object (material) of the faculty of desire as the determining ground of the will are without exception empirical and can hand down no practical laws" (Kant 1788: 38; 1993: 19). Kant distin-guishes between practical principles and practical laws or rules. Empirical principles, that is principles derived from experience, cannot serve to gener-ate rules in ethics, because this would imply that one's will would have some heteronomous determinant external to one's own desire; thus, we would not be able to make decisions freely. Although such a principle can become a subjective maxim, it can never provide the necessary objective and univer-sally valid rules for human conduct. Kant's basic rule for all moral action is as follows: "So act that the maxim of your will could always hold at the same time as a principle of universal law giving" (Kant 1788: 54; 1993: 30). In con-trast to the empirical principles underlying the doctrine of eudaemonism, a moral law must be a synthetic, *a priori* proposition, because will is deter-mined as "pure will", independent of empirical conditions and only by the form of the law itself. This determinant is seen as the ultimate condition underlying all maxims for conduct. Will is free; the law general. The law does not contain the will's determination in an intrinsic sense; rather, it reflects its basic form. Thus, Kant's categorical imperative demands the exclusion of competing subjective maxims.

The fascinating aspect of Kant's formalistic ethics lies in the fact that the "moral law" (*Sittengesetz*) itself becomes the deductive principle – namely, of volition – rather than that it be necessary to derive it from human ecological or other values. However, Kant does not wish to exclude values and practical principles; he simply wants to force them into the mould of a comprehensive systematique. Although, in accordance with his doctrine, Kant must prevent a mixing of concepts, he does not necessarily wish to maintain the real-world separation as well: "pure practical reason does not require that we should renounce the claims to happiness; it requires only that we take no account of them whenever duty is in question" (Kant 1788: 166; 1993: 97).

The systematic reason for the conceptual separation of moral law (ethics) and the doctrine of happiness (eudaemonism) is in reality the problem of the "highest good" (*höchstes Gut*). The moral law can *a priori* generate subjective maxims for conduct, but its meaning and purpose are not contained in them. Morality and happiness are united in the concept of the highest good as consummated good, in the sense that happiness always presupposes right action according to prescribed moral rules. This means that although we should indeed hope and strive for an improvement in the quality of life, this alone is not sufficient motivation to pursue the goal of a healthy environment and a balanced ecosystem.

Environmental ethics: meaning and alternative

Many objections have been raised to Kantian ethics. One of the sharpest criticisms came from Hegel, who even went so far as to refer to the categorical imperative as the principle of immorality, because it is merely formal and therefore open to every interpretation as regards its contents. The various formulations of the categorical imperative in Kant's *Grundlegung zur Metaphysik der Sitten* show, however, that this opinion is unfounded. Objectively, the basis for moral law lies in universality: "Act only on that maxim through which you can at the same time will that it should become a universal law" (Kant 1785: 421; 1993: 84). The corresponding difficulty with Kantian ethics is the application of the laws of reason to the sensory world, that is to concrete human action.

Subjectively, the basis of moral law (Pontius 1971: 123) is contained in every rational being (*Vernunftwesen*) as his/her subject and purpose: "Act in such a way that you always treat humanity,[1] whether in your own person or

---

1. "Humanity" (Menschheit) is not used here in the contemporary sense; it is best understood as "human being".

in the person of any other, never simply as a means, but always at the same time as an end (Kant 1785: 429; 1993: 91). We can derive social ethics and, therefore, environmental ethics from this variation of Kant's moral law. The question, then, is only whether it can transcend the form of individual ethics, that is whether it can escape the problem of ethical egocentricity. Since this is probably not the case, Kant's law cannot determine the goal of a collective ethical system, that is a system of social norms; nevertheless, it can establish the minimal conditions for such a system.

3.3 Green ethics – a political instrument?

"Ecologizing" cognition, behaviour and action

The human ecological elements in the academic disciplines can be drawn together to form a set, that is an integrative human ecology approach. Let us refer to this set of approaches as the "ecologization" of the sciences. If this is an inductive approach to human ecology, then a deductive one can be construed as follows. General systems theory and critical anthropology ask: What is the position of the human being with respect to the conditions of the social and ecological environment? They assume an inductive-synthetic approach of academic disciplines and unite in a common theory of human ecology.

One meta-justification for this approach comes from ethics and it proceeds from the assumption that scientists bear some responsibility towards society in terms of the consequences of their research. Thus, the search for appropriate explanations for and methods of control over the interconnections linking the economic and ecological cycles leads the scientist to think in terms of systems, and, thus, to incorporate a human ecological approach. The necessity for a meta-justification from ethics arises from the fact that the exact sciences cannot provide ethical norms – were they to attempt this, it would be tantamount to a so-called "naturalistic fallacy".

Environmental protection as the logical outcome of scientists' acting upon their responsibilities will place different degrees of emphasis conceptually or politically on protection of humans or nature conservation, both of which it encompasses. In every case, environmental actions resulting from relevant scientific findings must reflect "evolutionary strategies" between linear and network thinking. In this respect, changing ethical principles or adopting new ones is possibly less important than justifying social actions or adapting one's behaviour for nature's sake. Prevention, that is, the introduction of the time factor, plays an important role here.

We can discern three basic, but fundamentally different, attitudes towards environmental ethics:

- a new ethics is called for
- new action is called for; traditional ethics is sufficient
- no ethics is sufficient; a set of medium-scope rules for conduct is required, ranging from economic incentives to legal prohibitions.

The first variant demands new foundations for a new area of human responsibility. The second variant resists the instrumentalization of ethics for purposes of environmental protection, but it does not deny the legitimacy of a rational foundation. The third variant negates the rational context of foundation and legitimation, but in so doing, it overlooks the fact that although foundations may be disguised, they continue to exist implicitly. Thus, no matter how we choose to view it, in every case environmental or natural configurations rest upon an ethical issue: What should we want? Here, knowledge about systems interrelations compounds the problem more than has been traditionally necessary, making ecological or "ecologized" ethics, in view of complex ecological systems in general, even more artificial and more complicated.

Behavioural goals derive from ethics, not from science. Ethics deals with good and evil, right and wrong actions. Knowledge of this is assumed if one asserts that some given measure is better or worse than another. Implicit also in this assumption is that there must be some "best measure", whether or not it be known. In other words, the question of alternative measures is posed. In medicine this corresponds to therapeutic scope. But, whereas the medical field has been able to make use of the best available measures because of the existing system of national health and bonds of solidarity uniting the healthy with the sick, the field of environmental protection orientated towards nature conservation has had to reckon with opposing interests and finance policy restrictions. These factors dominate and determine the level of environmental protection. At this point, we are confronted with rational limitations that will be revealed through a critical examination of ideologies.

Ethics thus unites cognition and action; it is determined by goals, motives and impulses, which themselves proceed from notions of value. Measures must also take into account the current state of scientific knowledge; this also applies to ecological ethics. Limitations occur because of knowledge deficits (ecological knowledge), dependence upon vested interests, and (alleged) scarcity of means. Therefore, a corrective that takes a more critical approach is needed.

At this point, we have to add that human behaviour is, ethically speaking, accompanied by responsibility. Here as well a new dimension comes into play: a look into the future. Phylogenetically speaking, this means that a "sense of time" must have developed among our subjects. Environmental protection, for example, has not only an objective aspect to it, but also an intentional one that includes concept and deed. This applies analogously to every form of creativity and every form of culture. Environmental ethics is a product of this intentionality, which includes the idea of Utopia, a not yet existing form to be realized at some point in the future. The accompanying situational analysis includes the idea of "immediate context" with other living beings (*Mitwelt*). Thus, the surrounding outside world (*Außenwelt*) and the individual's immediate context (*Mitwelt*) make up the environment (*Umwelt*).

Short- and long-term strategies follow from the principle of responsibility. What is good can be decided "objectively" or "democratically": the human ecologist knows, but the majority decides what is to be done. Here, the old philosophical problem of right action rears its head once again. If learning, training and education transmit awareness of the problem and ecological knowledge, who, then, instructs the teacher? And, moreover, would this mean that ecological cognition and action are attained?

The following theses could apply to science and ethics. Even if ethics has, up to now, been a luxury, changed circumstances have made it a necessity. The essence of this change is that the means-to-ends relations in the context of technological and scientific development have become independent. This urgent situation compels science and ethics to work towards preserving free and right action in relation to the environment. This process is called "ecologization", which means that ecological thinking is not the exclusive property of any special discipline; it also enriches other disciplines through the introduction of networking and the principle of cycles in place of linearity and causality. Environmental policy decisions occur through individual and supra-individual decision-making processes, the consequences of which can be classified as desirable or undesirable, known or unknown. If the function of human ecology is to reduce the number of unknown consequences, then it is the function of ethics to reduce the number of undesirable ones. The relationship of that which is to that which ought to be is, unfortunately, often clouded by misunderstanding; and this leads directly to the naturalistic fallacies mentioned above.

The naturalistic fallacy trap in environmental ethics

For reasons that have to do with the logic of cognition, it is not possible to derive statements about what should be (ethical demands) from statements about what is. Ethical propositions cannot be established on the basis of scientific findings. This applies to the natural sciences and social sciences alike. Surprisingly, however, this knowledge that follows from simple, logical principles is often met with misunderstanding or even resistance, particularly among natural scientists who deal actively with environmental problems but who have never been forced to pause and reflect on the basic assumptions underlying their respective disciplines. This gives rise to the presumption that scientists can draw conclusions regarding norms and values from research findings, where, at the very most, they can only assert in the form of if–then statements that there is a set of limiting conditions. On the other hand, cognitive logic's separation of that which is from that which ought to be is often mistakenly taken to mean that scientists should not become engaged in themes that may interest them but which are outside the scope of their scientific disciplines, that is, that they should restrict themselves to the pursuit of value-free judgements.

It should be kept in mind that the claim that science and its findings are always value-free is itself ideological. At best we can acknowledge that attempts to achieve value-free results are conceivable. A completely different issue is whether or not science should be value-free. And if so (or if not), in which sense? An answer can certainly be given to this question, although the issue need not be inherent to science. Scientists should, therefore, engage themselves within the context of the research process for that which they consider to be good and right, without of course violating the recognized rules of the cognitive process. In short, norms enter into the scientific process constitutively as meta-assumptions. They are not derived from scientific processes. They are prerequisite but not inferable. And this is the decisive point where the confusion occurs.

To hold that demands must be based upon natural scientific statements is, in logic, to commit the naturalistic fallacy. On the other hand, the introduction of norms transcendental to science into the cognitive processes carries with it the hidden danger that science would be thus ideologized. The demand is, therefore, that constitutive norms be disclosed. To disguise or ignore them is ideology.

The naturalistic fallacy can be illustrated by an example from natural science. Ecology, as a natural science discipline, makes statements about the conditions that stabilize ecosystems, but it does not and cannot demand that ecosystems be stabilized. On the contrary, the fact of and necessity for permanent change is implicit in the idea of steady-state. Natural history in the sense of the evolutionary process "lives" from change, including, for instance, the extinction of less well-adapted species. In this sense, then, basic ethical demands to secure the continued existence of the human species or to preserve a given quality of life are not inferable from ecological or human ecological scientific results. According to the principles of ecology and the theory of evolution, then, there is absolutely no reason why the species *Homo sapiens*, in so far as it behaves like dinosaurs, should not end up like them.

What remains, then, is a justification for the demand that norms "foreign to science" should control cognitive processes, not in the sense of falsifying scientific results, but rather in the sense of structuring or designing research. Like all citizens, scientists are obliged to adhere to right conduct on the basis of given norms. This imperative comes from ethics, not from science. Unlike "Joe Average", however, scientists find themselves in a socially privileged position in virtue of their role in society and level of education, in so far as

70

they have more ready access to scientific contexts than most of the population. The scientists' knowledge theoretically puts them in a better position to see and understand the social changes and risks entailed by scientific developments. But this privileged position, made possible and financed by society, also burdens the scientists with more responsibility towards that society. An example of this is provided by nuclear physicists in Germany in the late 1930s who, once the uranium atom had been successfully split in the laboratory, were acutely aware that this technology made it possible to construct the atom bomb and who therefore acted to obstruct its production.

In sum, from this brief description of scientists' responsibility, we can see that there is in fact interaction between ethics and science, but this interaction springs from two separate sources. Moreover, this interaction becomes all the more important when we consider that Joe Average today can hardly discern what conduct is right in certain situations. The complexity of interrelations makes it more difficult to know what is right and to do what is right, and this dilemma itself forms a basic problem of environmental ethics.

Problems and paradoxes of environmental ethics

The basic problem for environmental ethics and, later on, for environmental policy is the determination of whether environmental protection should exist for the sake of humankind or whether it should exist for its own sake. One essential difference between ethical and political blueprints of earlier times and those of today lies in the fact that, in the past, the contexts of human actions were known. The ethical approach that aims at the individual could be confident that healthy, mature persons could know and had to know what was good and what was evil. If we observe the effects of human intervention into the ecosystem, we can see that this is no longer the case. The ecosystem, Earth, is not entirely known and cannot be controlled instrumentally. Although we are generally aware of the hazards of pollution, for instance, even ecosystem researchers are not able to predict with any degree of certainty what the impacts of individual interactions might be. Thus, in many cases the harmful effects of interventions into nature are difficult if not impossible to estimate. It is precisely because knowledge of the effects of technology is lacking – so goes the new argumentation – that there is the ethical demand to handle nature as carefully as possible, to intervene in the natural order as little as possible.

The ecological and long-term economic requirements for survival of society can be inferred from the principle of precaution. These requirements are "sold" to us in a variety of packages: social taboos, legal or incentive systems. They are based upon various interpretations of humankind's place in the environment. Various foundations, explanations, plausibilities and interpretations come to us through theology, philosophy, the physical sciences, ecol-

71

ogy, and those areas that are not exclusively contemplative-theoretical, such as religion, ethics and aesthetics.

Human ecology, as an action-orientated science, maintains that our knowledge of ecosystems does not match our ability to destroy the Earth. Human ecology describes and circumscribes a normative point of reference. Against the backdrop of responsibility for future generations, we can raise the question right now as to what environmental policy must look like 20 years hence. It is not difficult to maintain that environmental policy must have a global scope and, for instance, that it must be equally valid for Washington, Moscow, Rio de Janeiro or Dar es Salaam. With so many differing situations and interests at stake, however, the question of the validity, the "truth", of environmental policy is bound to be raised; but, because of lack of knowledge of contextual relations, it will be very difficult to answer this question adequately. In view of the 12000 million persons who will populate the Earth 20 years from now (a great number of whom will be threatened by starvation), philosophically speaking, the practical (as opposed to theoretical), hence the ethical justification of global environmental policy is becoming increasingly significant. Ethics is a sluggish output variable that has, up to now, always been running well behind the facts. The time has come for it to take the lead.

An antecedent description of norms would permit us to ascertain which norms are available and applied in environmental policy. At the descriptive level, we may still meet with the functional objection that we face a normative deficit that could be reduced by augmenting the original norms. Environmental ethics would then have to verify this augmentation by establishing its logical ethical foundations.

The normative structure of an environmental policy must develop further out of crises and catastrophes if society is to survive. The real or predicted occasions of this development include environmental pollution, which disrupts the entire economic system, global limits to economic growth, depletion of genetic stock, or nuclear war. In such cases, society's survival itself may become the highest value, from which, together with a set of additional supportive conditions, a material value ethics can be derived.

The starting point for an environmental ethical system is a critique of the instrumental relations between humans and the environment. In contrast to the anthropocentric ethical systems that have been so common throughout the history of philosophy, environmental ethics makes nature the object of human responsibility. This orientation touches human ecology, which is biocentric at its core. What both have in common is the quest for a social dimension. In the philosophical tradition, the ego was enthroned in knowledge (epistemology) and action (ethics). The domination-of-nature ideology arose out of the dissociation of cognition and action from ethical principles, and in the wake of the sheer success of science and technology. Two demands are consequent:

- moral action must become the power that regulates power itself
- for politics to be ecological, ethics must first incorporate an ecological perspective.

It must be borne in mind, however, that in attempting to achieve this objective, one can easily end up in a state of *aporia*. The existence of the world must conjointly represent its own value, which, in turn, justifies the norm that the existence of the world must be preserved. This means that that which is becomes that which ought to be: metaphysics becomes ethics. The weakness here, however, is that the justification for "humans and the world ought to exist" is missing. In light of this weakness in material value ethics, then, pleas in defence of formalistic environmental ethics take on increasing plausibility. In accordance with the Kantian model, contradiction-free foundation and derivability are given. The weakness, however, of a formal approach lies in the fact that consequences of and responsibility for actions are accorded far too little relevance. Whereas material environmental ethics has difficulty deriving imperatives, formalistic environmental ethics, although more elegant, completely neglects its material object, the environment (cf. Summerer 1989a).

Ultimately, these weaknesses lead to the collapse of environmental ethics or, at least, negate its claim to absoluteness. One solution is offered by the introduction of middle-range pragmatic rules to establish social environmental responsibility, spanning religious ritualization, economic incentives, legal directives and injunctions. Such rules have the advantage that they allow values to be weighed against one another – for instance, ecological values versus democratic values – and, in so doing, are better able to keep restrictions on freedom at a minimum and to prevent forms of "ecofascism" (e.g. euthanasia). On the other hand, this proposed solution only shifts the question of values and justification of actions to another level, and therefore it does not contribute to clarity and rationality in policy implementation.

3.4 Conclusion

Human ecological ethics has traditionally emphasized material values. However, general theory of value (Reichardt) contains several contradictions for which three possible resolutions exist. First, the assignment of a highest value is no answer in so far as material value theory *per definitionem* is based upon a hierarchy of values. Secondly, a casuistry of plausible arguments as a case-by-case pragmatic blueprint for action (Forrester, Randers and Meadows), because it adapts ethical standards to reality, runs the risk of adapting them affirmatively to "immoral" conditions as well. The third possible approach is formal ethics based upon Kantian concepts. This ethical system is characterized by autonomy of will, formalism and a priority. It replaces absolute values with absolute criteria for standards (maxims of the will). Although Kant's formalistic ethics attempts to achieve the stringency of natural law, it is nevertheless doubtful whether it can really transcend ethical egocentricity. Even if environmental ethics can be translated into a form of social ethics on this basis, we must remain sceptical as to the extent that this alone could contribute meaningfully to a reduction in environmental pollution.

What is required is a shift in society as a whole, especially in the domains of science and politics, towards ecological cognition and ecological behaviour. This implies large-scale cultural change (a widely discussed proposal, e.g. in Inglehart 1990) encompassing movement away from material values in northern industrialized societies, and a clear break with the perception of nature as a reserve that is at the disposal of the human being.

Concerning the role of ethics in this process, it is important to remember two things: ethics is a set of norms and not a political instrument; secondly, as a set of norms, ethics is not a part of science. These apparent weaknesses actually strengthen the independent position of ethics in the fields of science and politics. It may act as a social factor in its own right, which imposes the population's desire for ecological improvement on politics. Thus environmental ethics could play a part in attempts to alter the basic structure of legislative processes and economic policy measures. Here, environmental ethics surely has an important supplementary and even innovative task to fulfil. Legal and economic measures could mediate in harmonizing attitudes with actions, and individual desires with measures aimed at protecting the environment and ecological conservation.

Ultimately, though, we should be striving for a comprehensive ecologization of policy and policy areas, and not just the application of ecology as a lubricant that would facilitate the smooth running of the economic system. Reconciling economy and ecology may or may not prove illusory; this depends upon various constraints on the sociopolitical framework, such as available time, social dependencies, concepts of value, as well as control and regulatory mechanisms proper to the societal system itself.

CHAPTER 4
Environmental policy in Germany

"Environmental policy is the sum of all actions and activities aimed at preventing and avoiding encroachments on the environment, and at eliminating damage which has already occurred" (Hartkopf & Bohne 1983: 57). This definition of environmental policy was proposed by Eberhard Bohne and Günther Hartkopf; the latter was Secretary of State (*Staatsekretär*) under the German Federal Minister of the Interior from 1969 to 1983. During his 14 years in office, Hartkopf, considered to be the "father" of German environmental policy, was responsible for its continued rise and development.

The basic political principles of environmental protection in the Federal Republic of Germany (FRG) are those of precaution, the polluter pays and co-operation (Hartkopf & Bohne 1983: 71). The precaution principle means long-term orientation towards the future. It rests on the more fundamental principle of prevention. The polluter pays principle is designed to force those responsible for pollution to pay for its prevention or alleviation. The co-operation principle is meant to encourage a willingness to compromise with polluters in order to alleviate environmental damage; this principle is in part contrary to the first two.

4.1 Has environmental policy been successful thus far?

Origins in West Germany

The Constitution of the Federal Republic of Germany contains no provisions whatsoever relating to environmental protection, because environmental problems were not yet a political issue when the German Constitution (*Grundgesetz*) was being drawn up in the late 1940s. It is generally agreed that the German federal government is obliged to provide effective environmental protection, but whether or not this obligation can be inferred from the German Constitution – for instance, from articles concerning the "Dignity of Humans" or "Protection from Intervention by the State or Third Parties" – is still a matter of legal controversy. Environmental protection is only mentioned secondarily or tertiarily in terms of some specific areas of policy and legislation such as atomic energy (Hartkopf & Bohne 1983: 72–6; Weidner 1991: 142).

Since 1969–70, environmental protection in the FRG has come to be seen as an independent political task. The German federal government presented its first environmental programme in 1971. This programme was revised and updated with new points of focus in 1976 with the publication of the government's "Report on the Environment" (*Umweltbericht*). This new policy continued until the 1980s and was, according to Hartkopf & Bohne, largely successful. It stressed the following points:

- Protection from harmful biochemical and biophysical environmental effects was accorded priority over resource conservation.
- Priority was accorded to protecting human health; plants and animals were given less consideration.
- Protection was directed primarily towards environmental media (soil, water, air) and sectors (individual areas of application for specific substances); emphasis was placed accordingly on prevention or abatement of immediate environmental damage. An extension of protection to whole ecosystems, including cross-medial, cross-sectoral, and indirect environmental impacts, is still only in the initial stages of development.
- Efforts were concentrated mainly on improving and enacting legal regulations and less so on the problems of enforcement.
- Accordingly, the main emphasis was placed on directly effective regulations and prohibitions; indirect economic incentives were used only in isolated cases.
- Solutions for national problems had priority over international activities (Hartkopf & Bohne 1983: 85 f.).

But, has environmental protection in the FRG really been as successful as Hartkopf & Bohne seem to suggest? The number of critical voices has increased. In 1983and 1984, the then president of the German Federation for Environment and Nature Conservation (Bund für Umwelt und Naturschutz Deutschland – BUND), Hubert Weinzierl, declared "National Environment Day" to be a "day of mourning". In his declaration, he stated:

> . . . in view of the wasting away of forests, rivers and fields, National Environment Day in 1984 can, once again, only be celebrated as a day of deepest mourning. . . . Politics has not measured up to the task of leadership in environmental protection. (Weinzierl 1984)

These two judgements on almost two decades of German federal environmental policy are diametrically opposed. What standards were being used? What are the facts? What were the measures for control and regulation? The differing standards of judgement can be explained by the fact that in one case administrative and legislative environmental protection measures were assessed, whereas in the other case attention was concentrated on the most menacing problems, that is, precisely in those areas where environmental policy has failed. And indeed, of what use are "successfully" concluded programmes that prove to be effective only in limited areas, when the environment is exposed to far greater hazards than ever before?

Weinzierl (1984) estimated damages in the FRG for one year to amount to the following:

- *c.* 5000 ha of land are depleted
- at least one million hectares of forest begin to die back
- 1000 million trees die
- 60 000 tonnes of various toxic substances are released, and
- tens of thousands of persons become ill as a direct result of air pollution.

In light of these claims, it would indeed seem necessary to call into serious doubt the effectiveness of environmental policy as it has been carried out in the FRG thus far, despite a degree of success. Approximately one-third to one-half of all indigenous flora and fauna are threatened with extinction. The use of chemicals in agricultural production is so profuse that even those products that are grown without application of toxic substances, including so-called "toxic-free" or "natural" products, often contain residual amounts of dangerous substances. Incalculable amounts of dangerous substances are reaching us through the food chain. High levels of nitrate pollution in over-fertilized soils result in the eutrophication of freshwater lakes. Water treatment and purification still fail to measure up to the highest standards in accordance with the latest available technology. Hardly any effective measures have been implemented for combating air pollution, which is already having profound and disastrous effects on forests.

It is certainly no wonder, then, that the number of competent voices raised against German environmental policy has increased, accusing the government of treating symptoms rather than combating the causes (Meyer-Abich 1984a,b). Following the change in government in late 1982, some additional efforts were made in the area of environmental policy, particularly concerning air quality. In 1986, the German Federal Ministry for the Environment, Nature Conservation and Nuclear Safety (*Bundesministerium für Umwelt, Naturschutz und Reaktorsicherheit*), was established in the wake of the nuclear accident in Chernobyl and with a view towards the coming state elections in Lower Saxony at that time (Glaeser 1988: 65–7). Nevertheless, it cannot be claimed that the transition from the old social–liberal (Social Democratic Party–Free Democratic Party) coalition to a conservative Christian–liberal (Christian Democratic–Christian Socialist Union–Free Democratic Party) coalition government has brought about any significant change in German environmental policy.

The new government's environmental policy did, however, get off to a dynamic start and achieved some major breakthroughs in the late 1980s, having given priority to enforcement over planning. Klaus Töpfer, a regional planning professional and environmental expert, soon gained respect among experts and the general public when he took over the ministry in 1987 (until 1994). The first significant steps were the development of a concept for protecting the North and Baltic Seas and amendments to the laws on environmental liability in 1990. These included full liability for "inherited" ecological damage and a partial alleviation of the victim's burden of proof. Measures on controlling air and water quality soon had positive effects, although little influence could be achieved on EC/EU automobile exhaust policy. Likewise, groundwater and soil pollution and canopy die-back remained problem areas where little progress was made. Nuclear energy policy remained vulnerable and controversial. Policy on chemicals (the enforcement of the 1980 Chemicals Act) and hazardous waste came in for sharp criticism (cf. Weidner 1991: 142–3). On the whole, the environmental policy pursued by the German government since 1986 was considered progressive by outsiders, whereas at home not all that much was achieved. However, whereas there were obvious shortcomings, it must be remembered that the intensive coverage in the press and other news media of ecological issues, and the keen environmental awareness of the German public tend to emphasize failures rather than successes.

Environmental policy after unification

After what was called the "peaceful revolution" in Autumn 1989, the information disclosed on the catastrophic ecological conditions in the former GDR astounded West German experts. Collaboration on environmental issues was immediately intensified (the West German government had already provided support, including financial aid of 300 million Deutschmark, for six pilot projects in the GDR in July 1989). With formal reunification on 3 October 1990, co-operation based on partnerships came to an end; West German environmental laws (and EC/EU regulations: cf. Bruckmeier, Glaeser & Grund 1995) were adopted by the five new federal states, transition periods notwithstanding. The goal was to establish the "cornerstones for ecological restoration and development in the new states" by the year 2000 (BMU 1991). The dramatic economic slump that followed unification makes it highly unlikely that this target will be reached. In addition, transferring and institutionalizing the complex West German legal and administrative systems is in itself an extremely time-consuming process.

Long-standing and effective instruments for environmental protection in the former GDR received no support after unification and collapsed; one example is "SERO", the waste collection and recycling system (which was converted into a private stock company in 1995). Public participation in planning procedures was curbed in order to accelerate industrial and public development projects (cf. Weidner 1995: §3.3). All in all we can state that western Germany dominates eastern Germany in a quasi-imperialistic fashion, with the result that opportunities provided by the reunification process for a remodelling of institutional, legal and administrative structures, including environmental policy, were lost.

Comparative evaluation

Independent environmental organizations rated German environmental policy (before unification) as the best among a group of Western nations:

> An international coalition of more than 150 environmental groups . . . said Western Germany leads the group of seven industrialized countries in protecting the environment . . . based on their actions in six areas – global climate change and energy, biodiversity, ocean pollution, population, environmental aid to Eastern Europe, and "global environmental bargaining", or sustainable development aid to the Third World. (*International Environment Reporter*, July 1990: 28. For a critical evaluation in an international comparison of 24 countries, see Jänicke & Weidner 1995)

As far as conventional, reactive environmental policy goes, Germany's record is at least above average. If we compare trends in environmental quality and emissions, German achievements are among the best in the world, comparable to countries like Japan, Sweden, Switzerland and the Netherlands. This is true for figures on the availability of technologies that reduce sulphur dioxide (SO_2) and nitrogen oxides (NO_x) emissions, the proportion of lead-free petrol and low-pollution cars, the permissible levels for air pollutants (including dioxin from waste incineration plants), and waste incineration at sea. Discharge of liquid waste into the North Sea ceased in 1989. Germany is also a leader in sewage purification and will be among the first nations to halt production and use of chlorinated fluorocarbons (CFCs) and ban dioxin-forming additives (scavengers). The 1991 Packaging Ordinance obliges the manufacturing, retailing and packaging sectors to take back all wrappings and containers from the consumer and recycle them. A proposed levy on carbon dioxide (CO_2) emissions has been blocked in expectation of a corresponding EC/EU directive (cf. Weidner 1991: 148–50; Weidner 1995: §5.2).

4.2 Political implementation

The basic shortcomings of environmental policy as it has been practised up to now in Germany can be summarized as follows (Hartkopf & Bohne 1983: 86):

79

- insufficient resource protection
- insufficient protection of flora and fauna
- insufficient protection of ecosystems, and
- insufficient enforcement.

What is missing is an environmental policy that extends over media and sectors, which recognizes dangers early on, and which successfully implements relief measures. The basis of such a policy is clarity over what values are to be pursued. The first step, then, in trying to justify an environmental policy would be to render implicit values explicit, rather than trying to further conceal them. Only on this basis can general environmental awareness be strengthened politically. This should not be confused with political indoctrination, however, as that would violate other basic legal and welfare state values. Both ecofascism and ecostalinism are to be rejected.

Functionalistic environmental legislation that treats only symptoms falls too short of the goal. The introduction of values and their ethical justification are important here. Politically, this means judging values comparatively and openly, and making the resultant evaluation the basis of political consensus. Opponents of environmental policy measures (for example the German automobile industry, which, up to 1985, held proponents of the catalytic converter at bay by engaging in protracted discussions over reductions in automobile emissions) would then be forced to present their case on the same fundamental level.

Preventive environmental policy in this broad, but fundamental sense means not only nature conservation policy, but also social, economic (Binswanger 1989, Leipert 1989) and land-use planning policy (Fürst 1989) as well. These policies can then be said to operate successfully if they result in an ecologization of policy in general and if they promote industrial state "ecodevelopment". This would go far beyond the reductionist approach, which has dealt with environmental media and economic sectors separately. Thus each specific policy area could be given a human ecological "lining" to its own perspective. At the same time, we must ask whether, with a renewed retreat to sectoral policy, the human ecological demand is not altogether eliminated from the outset. The answer to this question will be negative for this reason: even though only one policy provides the starting point for implementation, the customary approach is nevertheless expanded to include the goal of ecologizing each respective sectoral policy. It is exactly this process that represents the implementation of the human ecological paradigm in a preventive environmental policy based upon a more varied, but nevertheless more concrete, arrangement of details.

Medial (soil, water, air) environmental policy is based upon a narrow, reductionist environmental concept, and thus it exhausts itself in simply dealing with symptoms. This can be seen in the examples of planning, which miss the target completely in terms of those directly affected. The first requirement for planners, therefore, should be the reconstruction of the world-views of those affected. The second requirement should be to maintain or to regain the affected individuals' power to act. One way to achieve this aim would be to include those affected in the planning process. Here, the same principles appear to apply for urban planning (Schubert 1989) as they do for agricultural planning in rural areas (Kölsch 1989), and for the industrialized world (Fischer 1989) as well as for developing countries (Teherani-Krönner 1989).

Environmental policy is not, however, subject only to politico-administrative control. It is also dependent upon technological development, which, in turn, is steered by vested interests and power establishments. This means that technology rules, that is, that the experts exercise domination over those affected (expertocracy). This conflict of interests has never been so clear as it was during the transition from smaller scale to large-scale technologies, as exemplified by the development of large-scale power plants. Here, the simple cost–benefit relation between the local level (site) and the supra-regional level (consumers) has become reversed: those affected at the local level are forced to bear all the burdens of environmental pollution from emissions to degradation of the landscape but, at the same time, they benefit only minutely from the increased energy production capacity. Democratic and ecological values are congruent here, although it must be borne in mind that these are the values of an "economic minority". This minority will only become more powerful politically when environmental protection in the sense of nature conservation can be reproduced in the form of protecting human health in the sense of preserving the human race. Good health has attained such a high social value that its protection and support are almost always politically feasible. One possible reason for this could be that protection of human health has been supported over the years by such power lobbies as the medical association, the pharmaceuticals industry, and municipal and state hospitals.

In contrast to health policy, which is aimed directly at humans (Tretter 1989), to ecologize policy in the sense of developing a preventive environmental policy would mean closing material cycles and reducing the amounts of "waste materials" generated (Fischer 1989). In so doing, consideration must be given to the fact that neither nature nor future generations are able to articulate their needs. The task of preventive environmental policy – in so far as this has any meaning whatsoever and is feasible (for opposing views, see Kirsch 1989, Weichhart 1989c) – would be, therefore, to assume responsibility for nature and future generations and, at the same time, not allow environmental ethics to degenerate into some sort of residual ethics based upon individual persons (Summerer 1989b).

4.3 Unanswered questions concerning the society–environment system

Of course, it is easy to complain about the failures of policies, particularly in those areas where the natural and societal contexts have not been sufficiently understood. Ever since the organization of the human species into societies and states, interaction between the human species and natural systems has been virulent. It is, to a certain extent, a metabolic exchange process that connects social systems to their natural or near-natural environment, or separates them from it, as is made more apparent by increasing technical potential. Does this spell co-operation or confrontation between humans and nature? The search for human ecological rules, the society–environment system, only leads us to the theoretical foundations for a policy towards the environment. But every approach to this system generates more questions than answers.

Are there any society–environment systems that, in contrast to those with which we are already acquainted, function without disturbance? In order to affirm this question empirically, it is necessary to determine in what way such a system would differ from ours. Pre-industrial societies are usually cited as examples of such undisrupted systems. A supposed characteristic of these societies is that their ecological rules and control mechanisms are not derived from natural science, but rather from transcendent religious values (Weichhart 1989a,b).

What is the importance of time horizons, for instance, election cycles, a factory manager's considerations of long- or short-term profit maximization, the modern farmer *qua* agriculturalist's considerations of long- or short-term income maximization in contrast to the traditional farmer's preserving the land to hand down to future generations? The evolutionary transformation of nature, which also entails the extinction of various species over longer periods of time, stands in sharp contrast to the rapid anthropogenic changes of very recent decades, which pose a fundamental threat to species diversity.

What meaning, then, should be attached to demands to prohibit irreversible interventions into natural processes? According to the Second Law of Thermodynamics, natural processes are always irreversible, one example of this being the extinction of the dinosaurs long before the appearance of humans on this Earth. Natural history and the evolution of the species are always irreversible. Where can we draw the line? By what criteria? Which ethical demands are necessary, justifiable and inferable?

On the other hand, is all that is good ecologically also good in an ethical sense? Euthanasia proceeds from the dictate that humankind should ensure its survival by strengthening its healthy members and, in so doing, it makes use of an ecological principle. Is it, however, ethically acceptable (Summerer 1989a)?

We are confronted here with the problem of goal and value conflicts, complicated further by the introduction of ecological complexity (Fietkau 1989). Ecological and social values conflict with one another; social ethical values conflict with individual ethical values. One example of these sorts of conflicts, which has become highly visible politically, is the antagonism between ecology and economy, which has resulted in an "unholy" alliance between capital and labour to oppose the safeguarding of ecological interests. In the forefront is the lowest common denominator: protecting jobs (Leipert 1989). What social cover-ups are playing a role here?

Political development in past years has shown that ecological and human ecological principles can be incorporated into almost any world-view, any ideology, or any sociopolitical schema. Does this imply something like ecological arbitrariness? Is the answer to this question negative, in so far as the various ontological, ideological sociopolitical currents use arguments based on ecologically orientated values, which are in fact logical reflections or derivatives of one another? What does it mean when ecological values and eco-movements can no longer be forced into a traditional political left–right schema?

A partial answer to these questions may lie in the fact that the concept of ecology, the science of the interaction of various species, was developed out of biology, and that the notion of human ecology came about only after a reinterpretation of "ecology" by social scientists and other scholars of the humanities (Huber 1989). One difference between an ecological approach and a human ecological approach most certainly lies in the nature of systems regulation. In the one case, the focus is on immanently existing goals; in the other, the focus is on autonomous, system-transcendent goals. The control of human societies, including their environmental interactions, is in accord with the latter model and occurs through the use of political, economic and social mechanisms (Fischer 1989). Human ecological models are complex and, up to now, they have been investigated almost exclusively in pre-industrial societies. In the present context, however, industrial societies and their susceptibility to human ecological influence in various areas of policy have come to the fore of the agenda.

4.4 Conclusion

The prevailing environmental policy in Germany (as in other countries) has been one that favours reactive and remedial measures over a preventive approach and has been limited to sectoral issues rather than playing a central role in the entire political framework. Nevertheless, this policy could be implemented much more effectively in the 1980s than in the 1970s. Continuity as opposed to change – despite a switch in government – may seem surprising, but indicates that party politics has little significance when it comes to environmental matters. A similar result will be found with respect to China (see Ch. 5). Recently revised liability laws, efforts to reduce CO_2 emissions and the Packaging Ordinance provide examples for an ecological reorientation of environmental policy towards addressing causes of pollution and husbanding resources in general. German environmental policy received greater appreciation from international observers than from the German public; the latter are far more critical of shortcomings and failures because they are felt more immediately in a country with a particularly high density of population, industry, traffic and transportation.

As for the future of environmental policy in Germany, the outlook must be rather pessimistic due to the deplorable environmental and economic situation in eastern Germany, where the catching-up process competes with environmental tasks and hinders the political influence of environmental movements.

PART THREE
Implementation: two examples

CHAPTER 5

Environment and development in China: problems and policies

China has suffered severe environmental problems in urban industrial and rural areas, but has pursued an environmental policy that has remained surprisingly consistent despite significant changes in China's political situation. Unfortunately, China has also been consistent in its failure to fully implement all of the environmental measures proposed over the years. China contributed significantly to the ecodevelopment approach – that is, to environmental sustainability – because it has maintained the conviction that environmental considerations are an integral part of development policy. But just as development policy in China since 1949 has oscillated between a strategy of distribution first and then growth and growth first and then distribution, there has also been a double tradition of gentle adjustment and massive transformation in relation to nature and environment.

This chapter will investigate Chinese environmental policy from 1949 to the present, with reference to the specific problems that have existed and continue to exist. These include air, water and soil pollution, energy use, and the environmental consequences of the steadily increasing already vast population. The cultural tradition underlying China's approach to environmental policy will be discussed, likewise the increased awareness of global environmental issues and China's willingness to participate at an international level to help alleviate more than just domestic problems, particularly since the Stockholm Conference in 1972.

The database for an overall survey of environmental problems in China, in sharp contrast to other areas of information, is very weak. Until 1978, very little was published or released on environmental issues; one was forced to rely on piecemeal information, such as what one could glean from travel reports or similar documents. Despite China's greater openness after 1978, macro-geographical data are still not available, and a state of the environment report for China does not exist.

The limited database leaves wide scope for evaluation and interpretation of environmental problems and policies in China. In general, earlier Western writings tended to picture a Maoist paradise based upon a successfully implemented, autocentred, decentralized development strategy – a blissful world of cheerful people thriving in a healthy, sound environment. By the 1980s, however, the pendulum had begun to swing the other way. Massive failures in developmental policy were uncovered – poverty, famines, unemployment, and an environment "in poor shape and still deteriorating" (Smil 1984: xii). This chapter attempts to steer a course between Scylla and Charibdis, taking account of the grave socio-economic and ecological problems in this developing country as well as, on the other hand, acknowledging those environmental policies contained in China's development strategy and designed to improve the situation.

5.1 Environmental problems and policies 1949–78

Types of environmental problems

China faces similar rural and urban environmental problems to other developing countries. Within the past 30 years, at least a quarter of China's forests have been felled; since 1957 one-third of the total arable land has been lost to agricultural production; harmful chemicals are deposited in soil and water; in Chinese cities, air, water and noise pollution have reached discomforting levels (see Fig. 5.1 and Schaffer 1986: 735–7); waste disposal and traffic problems are increasing.

AIR POLLUTION

Air pollution, mainly in the form of smog and dust, plagues most urban areas and industrial centres. The major sources of air pollution are industrial production processes and coal-based energy production. Other sources, however, are the winds that carry dust from the deserts of Inner Mongolia and the loess plateau to the northern settlements. In so far as soil erosion, the main cause of dust on the loess plateau, is a result of deforestation, this type of pollution can be classified as anthropogenic as well.

In 1986, 24 million tonnes of sulphur dioxide (SO_2) and 22 million tonnes of dust ($2.3 t/km^2$) were registered; threshold values are frequently exceeded. In Beijing, for instance, the situation is made particularly deplorable by low chimneys. They account for the high SO_2 ground concentration during times of atmospheric thermal inversion (smog). Four-fifths of all emissions are caused by the combustion of low quality coal in power plants, industrial boilers, steam locomotives, ships and household stoves. Heavy industry is another source of emissions. Particularly heavily polluting industries are iron and steel mills, colour metallurgy, refineries, chemical plants and cement manufacture. A steadily increasing number of motor vehicles can be expected to worsen the situation.

1	Harbin	2	Changchun	3	Shenyang
4	Beijing region	5	Hohot	6	Tiayuan
7	Jinan	8	Lanzhou	9	Xian
10	Zhengzhou	11	Shanghai region	12	Wuhan
13	Chengdu	14	Changsha	15	Guangzhou
16	Kunming	17	Chongqing		

Figure 5.1 Centres of pollution in China. *Source:* Schaffer (1986: 736).

The obvious effects of air pollution in China have been an increase in lung cancer mortality among humans, and acid rain damage and photochemical smog affecting crops and other plants (Smil 1984: 114–26; Schaffer 1986: 744–9; Betke 1989: 64–8).

WATER POLLUTION
China's rivers carry many kinds of toxic pollutants from industrial waste water. Pollutants include organic wastes, oil products, chlorinated hydrocarbons, nitrates, sulphates, phenolic compounds, cyanides, arsenic and heavy metals such as lead, chromium, cadmium and mercury. Coal-fired power plants emit 15 million tonnes of ash annually into Chinese rivers. Most polluted waters are concentrated in and around cities. Polluting industries tend

88

to be relocated in rural areas, where the toxic waste waters they emit are frequently channelled into irrigation systems. China's total irrigated area comprises nearly 0.5 million km^2. Waste water is estimated to amount to a total of 60 million m^3, only 8 per cent of which is treated.

In Shanghai, drinking water is taken from the Suzhou and Huangpu Rivers. These rivers receive four million tonnes of industrial and household wastes daily, only 4 per cent of which are treated. The result is that enormous quantities of chlorine are added to drinking water. Fish cannot survive in waters within urban limits, groundwater reserves are overtapped and the phreatic water table is sinking at a rate of up to 0.5 m annually. Beijing alone required an estimated 600–800 million m^3 drinking water from groundwater reservoirs in 1990 (Smil 1984: 100–13; Schaffer 1986: 739–43; Betke 1989: 61–4).

SOIL DEGRADATION

Between 1957 and 1977, 210 000 km^2 of new agricultural land was reclaimed. Arable land has always been scarce in China, with only 1 million km^2 (10 per cent of the total land area) being used for agriculture. The newly recovered agricultural land is of poorer than arable quality; agricultural yields are at maximum only one-third of the Chinese average output.

In the same period, 1957–77, 330 000 km^2 or one-third of the previously cultivated prime arable soil (and since then about 7570 km^2 annually) was lost in part as a result of natural disasters, but also as a result of intensified development in rural and urban areas, including the construction of irrigation canals, water reservoirs, new roads, settlements and new factories. The population increased dramatically during this period. Between 1981 and 1984, in Beijing alone some 22.3 million m^2 of new floor area were established.

The quantitative decrease in land has been aggravated by qualitative decline. Forty per cent of China's total arable land consists of low-grade soils: 20 per cent is thin-layered hillside soil subject to erosion; 9 per cent is sandy soil; 8 per cent is waterlogged lowland and saline-alkaline soil; 3 per cent is low-grade paddy field. Such poor quality land has a yield capacity of only some 0.75–1.5 tonnes of grain per hectare per year.

Some cropping practices have also contributed to soil deterioration. Careless irrigation, for instance, has increased the salinity and alkalinity of soils on the Huabei Plain. It has also turned arable land in Hunan, Jiangsu and Guangdong into bog or gley soils. Other adverse cropping practices include the failure to rotate crops (for example continuous double or triple cropping of rice), replacing organic manure with chemical fertilizer, the failure to alternate between wet and dry crops, and reduced application of green manure and nitrogen-fixing legumes. Deficient soils with a shallow layer of humus do not respond to increased inputs of fertilizer and water (Smil 1984: 68–77; Schaffer 1986: 751–3; Betke 1989: 68–70).

Public health and environmental conditions

In the light of these tremendous ecological problems, which also had a destabilizing effect on society, China began to implement environmental policies at an amazingly early stage. Currently, Chinese environmental policy more or less follows the example of the Western industrialized nations, although in its earlier phases the approach was different (Glaeser 1990, 1991). Discussions on China usually see the year 1978, when the Cultural Revolution ended and the policy of modernization began, as marking a change in era; this will also be the case in the following analysis.

The Chinese revolution of 1949 was a revolution in an underdeveloped country whose population consisted predominantly of impoverished peasants. The position of the Chinese communists in the cities was rather weak, but, more than anyone else, it was urban dwellers who suffered most from the war, the destruction of industries and the ensuing economic crisis. The result was hunger, criminality and corruption in the cities. Under these circumstances, therefore, the Chinese government decided to rebuild the industrial capacities and improve the social situation of the urban proletariat. Medical care was part of this scheme, and it was within this context that the concept of "environmental hygiene" (*huanjing weisheng*) was developed. The provision of clean water was particularly promoted as a means to combat the rapid spread of disease and epidemics in cities.

Although the first environmental measures were designed to eliminate hygienic problems in urban residential areas, the environmental impacts of industrial production were not recognized until the first Five-Year Plan (1953–7). The main aim of this plan, implemented between 1955 and 1958, was to accelerate industrial production, particularly in heavy industries. This development pattern fitted the model of the Soviet centrally planned economy, and it was heavily subsidized by Soviet aid. As a result, the urban population grew from 10.6 per cent in 1949 to 12.5 per cent in 1952 and 15.4 per cent of the total Chinese population in 1957.

The first Five-Year Plan did not mention the environmental impacts of industrialization, but it postulated, as an economizing principle, the use of natural resources sparingly and the recycling of resources gleaned from industrial waste. The principle of "multi-purpose use" (*zonghe liyong*) had an environmental impact, and in the early 1970s it was introduced as a fundamental principle of Chinese environmental policy (Sternfeld 1984: 7–8).

Research and laws established in the first Five-Year Plan

Scientific investigations in the 1950s showed that even at that time environmental problems were manifest. The main topics were air and water pollution, the ecological impacts of waste-water irrigation, environmental problems related to housing construction and city planning, and occupational diseases (Wang 1959). In particular, the impacts of air pollution on health were studied in Shanghai, Beijing, Qingdao, Tianjin and the industrial centres of the northeast, Shenyang, Fushun, Anshan and Lüda. According to some sources, the average SO_2 concentration in the industrial area of Tiexi in the city of Shenyang was nine times higher than that in comparable areas. A paint factory in Dalian emitted chlorine gas whose concentration was 8.8 times higher than the threshold values established at that time in the Soviet Union. An investigation among pupils in Fushun showed that these children were ill ten times more often than children living in cleaner environments. Many seven to thirteen year-olds living in the vicinity of a steel mill in Shijingshan showed a tendency to develop enlarged livers. The illness rates in this area were attributed to high concentrations of SO_2.

In 1956, several regulations and new laws were enacted to protect the health of industrial workers and the urban population in general. This legislation ruled that industrial facilities should not be sited upstream or in the main wind direction of residential areas. It called for the introduction of emission abatement technologies and ruled that industries could not be sited in water-protection zones. These regulations were enforced by the local health authorities and some initial achievements were registered in the late 1950s (Sternfeld 1984: 8–11).

From the "Great Leap Forward" to the "Cultural Revolution"

The "Great Leap Forward" (1958–62) propagated a massive development thrust by means of combined agricultural and industrial development in rural areas within "people's communes". From the environmental point of view, the value of these small and not always professionally managed production units was doubtful. The campaign was discontinued due to planning errors, natural catastrophes and the politically motivated withdrawal of Soviet development aid to China.

Immediately following the Great Leap, more environmental regulations were drawn up, particularly some maximum value regulations. These were among the first such standards in the world. During the early phase of the Cultural Revolution (1966–9), the environmental concept as established in the 1950s was basically given up. Self-reliance meant independence from imports, whereas mass mobilization was to be the motor of development. Environmental campaigns, which also made use of mass mobilization, were nevertheless initiated. One such campaign was called for by the Shanghai Revolutionary Committee to clean up the Huangpu and Suzhou Rivers:

> 90000 persons were mobilized on the industrial and agricultural fronts in Shanghai to form muck-dredging and muck-transporting teams,

waging a vehement people's war to dredge muck from Suzhou River. After 100 days of turbulent fighting, more than 403,600 tonnes of malodorous organic mire had been dug out. (New China News Agency, 21 October, 1969)

This drive was more likely motivated by economic reasons, however, than by ecological considerations. In the early 1970s, still during the Cultural Revolution, there was a definite change in environmental attitudes and policy, most probably influenced by discussions in the West such as the "limits to growth" debate. Ecology became a political topic and its emphasis shifted from issues of public health to ecosystem-related environmental protection. Accordingly, the term "environmental hygiene" was abandoned and replaced with the Western term "environmental protection" (*huanjing baohu*). This development coincided with China's opening up politically and economically, which resulted in new imports of technology after 1972, followed by industrial growth in 1973. This was also the year when Deng Xiaoping was reinstated – his first rehabilitation after seven years' denunciation. In 1975, Zhou Enlai proclaimed the "Four Modernisations" programme in industry, agriculture, science and technology, and defence (Sternfeld 1984: 11–15).

Campaigns on industrial waste and multi-purpose use

During the early 1970s, the campaign to recycle the "three industrial wastes" (*san fei*), solid waste, waste water and waste gas, resurrected the concept of multi-purpose use from the 1950s, but changed its emphasis from an economically orientated to an ecologically orientated principle. Multi-purpose use was enforced mainly in the steel, chemical, sugar and paper industries (Yu 1975), and the Chinese media reported extensively on new recycling methods. Some authors tended to interpret the successful recycling programmes and projects as part of the Chinese cultural heritage, as the traditional form of ecologically sound interaction between society and nature (e.g. Chin 1980, originally written in 1943) – a notion that was strengthened primarily by Joseph Needham (1954–86). Following this interpretation, recycling, for instance, as a basic principle of traditional agricultural technology (e.g. using human excrement as dung fertilizer), was transferred to modern industrial production.

In other sources, however, multi-purpose use was attributed less to Daoist philosophy and its strive towards harmony with nature than it was to Marxist natural dialectics (e.g. Yu 1987b): environmental protection vanquished the contradiction between economy and ecology. Good and bad were considered relative values and the campaign for multi-purpose use propagated the tenets of "converting wastes into valuables" (*bian fei wei bao*) and "converting the harmful into the beneficial" (*bian hai wei li*).

It is fairly obvious that Maoist ecological theory and campaigns were, to some extent at least, designed to serve the political and economic interests of the Maoist faction – that is, to strengthen an independent, autarkic economy. Although lack of economic resources motivated the multi-purpose use campaign, it is doubtful, according to some experts, whether it contributed to alleviating the growing ecological crisis (Schenkel 1982; Sternfeld 1984: 15–20).

Growth of international participation and institutional consequences in China

China, in common with many other countries, considered the 1972 UN conference in Stockholm to be the spring-off point for its own national environmental policy. The Chinese delegation submitted the following statement:

> In the developing countries, most of the environmental problems are caused by underdevelopment . . . Therefore the developing countries must mainly direct their efforts to develop their national economy, build their modern industry, and their agriculture, . . . to adequately solve their own environmental problems . . . (Sternfeld 1984: 22; cf. the altered version in UNCHE 1973: 17)

This formulation was changed slightly and added to Clause 4 of the final version of the Declaration on the Human Environment.

Whereas in the past, environmental policy measures were motivated by economic or developmental needs, here environment and development were explicitly related to one another and the solutions to problems in one area were inextricably linked to solutions to problems in the other. This must, therefore, be considered to be one of the origins of ecodevelopment, which was to be promoted by the UN Environment Programme, the UN agency founded in Nairobi as a result of the Stockholm conference.

On a national scale, China began to implement ecodevelopment principles by convening the First National Environment Conference in 1973 in Beijing. Policy guidelines for environmental protection were drawn up at this conference; environmental administrations at local, provincial and national levels were set up, and environmental research institutions were established (Sternfeld 1984: 23–30).

Qu Geping, then Deputy Director of the Bureau of Environmental Protection of the State Council (who may be called the "father" of Chinese environmental policy), stressed the preventive element to environmental protection in guidelines and policy statements, maintaining that environment and economic development had to be co-ordinated – which in fact is a restatement of the basic principle of ecodevelopment.

5.2 Environmental problems and policies after 1978

Economic reforms, readjustment policies and environmental impacts

The era following Deng Xiaoping's (second) rehabilitation in 1977 was characterized by availability of information and a more pragmatic, non-Maoist approach to development. In short, "readjustment" became the catchword of the post-Maoist period after 1978, heralding a new era of social and economic reforms. The Chinese mass media began to publicize the environmental policy concept drawn up in 1973 at the First National Environment Conference. Reports began appearing for the first time on severe environmental damage. At the same time, other "sensitive" issues were also receiving media attention for the first time, such as regional famines, unemployment rates and criminality. Environmental policy became an integral part of the so-called Four Modernisations Programme. An environmental protection clause was added to the Chinese Constitution (Article 11), thus making protection of the environment a state and governmental obligation. Finally, in September 1979 the Fifth National People's Congress adopted the Environmental Protection Law of the People's Republic of China for trial implementation (Anon. 1979; Glaeser 1983b: 9–28). This law was

> ... established in accordance with Article 11 of the Constitution ... which provides that "the State protects the environment and natural resources and prevents and eliminates pollution and other hazards to the public". (Environmental Protection Law, Article 1)

The function of the law is

> ... to ensure, during the construction of a modernized socialist state, rational use of natural environment, prevention and elimination of environmental pollution and damage to ecosystems, in order to create a clean and favourable living and working environment, protect the health of the people and promote economic development" (ibid.: Article 2).

Article 6 of the Environmental Protection Law incorporated a principle of Western environmental policy, namely, "whoever causes pollution shall be

responsible for its elimination". Article 18 imposes a fine for exceeding pollution standards. Article 32, Paragraph 1, imposes fines for violation of the
law; Paragraph 2 provides for making violation of the law a criminal offence.

While all of this sounded very promising, a major, and to Western observers familiar, problem arose – namely, implementation. This difficulty was
publicized in the Chinese press and, as a consequence, in 1981 the adjustment policy was strengthened and environmental protection was made a
mandatory part of development policy. The areas in which the law was most
strictly enforced suggest where it was that Chinese leaders thought the main
sources of environmental problems to be: construction projects for heavy
industry and manufacturing, mining, water management and water-related
construction projects, including canal digging and power plant construction,
city planning projects and urban renewal. Environmental impact statements
were prepared for 60 such construction projects between 1980 and 1983.
Urban development and urban renewal projects began to include the instal-
lation of waste treatment facilities. Fines were levied for emitting pollutants
above a certain standard and for improper disposal of solid and liquid
wastes. Fines were reported not only against production units, but against
managers as well – this is to be seen in the context of economic reform and
applying the principle of direct responsibility (Sternfeld 1984: 32–45).

Industry and energy

Doubts have been raised as to the efficiency of the industrial reforms and
their environmental impacts. In the late 1970s the Chinese industrial sector
was divided as follows on the basis of size, state ownership or collective
ownership of enterprises (*Bejing Review*, 18 March 1980). There were 48 000
large-scale, state-owned industries; 264 000 collectively owned, local (provincial and county) level enterprises; and 1.5 million small-scale, collectively owned businesses in the countryside. Experimental reforms in the
economic administrative system affected only some 7 000 state-owned industries; 56 per cent of all industrial enterprises had no part in this experiment
at all. Reforms within the top 4 per cent were slowed down by government
and after 1981 little information on the experiment was reported in official
Chinese publications.

The reason for the failure of the industrial reforms is seen by economic
observers to lie in the increased autonomy enjoyed by individual enterprises.
Too much autonomy tends to be dysfunctional in an economic system with
only limited price and market mechanisms. Solving environmental problems
cannot be left to individual or autonomous enterprises; it must be part of a
national movement that includes a broad spectrum of reforms, not limited to
government, ranging from politics to education. The industrial reforms
undertaken, however, seemed to be orientated only towards microeconomic

policy – a basis too small for the efficient implementation of environmental protection measures (Yu 1987a: 120–26).

The results of inefficient implementation of environmental policy can clearly be seen in China's urban industrial areas. Here, air pollution, the most prominent environmental problem, is energy related. Although China's annual average energy consumption amounts to some 850 million tonnes hard coal equivalent (HCE), less than double West Germany's annual average energy consumption, dust emissions in China, amounting to 14 million tonnes annually, are more than 15 times higher than West Germany's. China's SO_2 emissions, 15 million tonnes per annum, are four times higher than West Germany's. China's comparatively worse air pollution problem is in part due to the quality of coal used, where coal combustion represents 51 per cent of primary energy consumption in that country. In addition, overall energy-use efficiency in China is very low, only about 27 per cent, compared to 40 per cent or more in Western industrialized countries (Kinzelbach 1987: 174–7). For the Chinese leadership, this discrepancy demonstrates the clear need for industrial modernization. Moreover, it explains why economic inefficiency in the industrial sector is so strongly linked to implementation problems in pollution alleviation efforts: in China, energy is wasted.

Table 5.1   Data on the air quality of Chinese cities.

Location	SO_2 (mg/m³)	Dustfall (t/km²/ month)	Dust concentra- tion (mg/m³)	Type of data
Beijing	0.20	38	0.87	Average for the heating period in 1978
Shanghai	0.08–0.17	44–1822	0.28–0.54	Yearly average for 1977 in different parts of the city
Shenyang	0.087	38.5	0.512	Yearly average for 1978
Chongqing	0.21–0.78	13.5–30.5	0.46–2.02	Daily averages for February and March 1980
Lanzhou	0.25	35.9	1.32	Average for the heating period in 1978
Taiyuan	0.24	35	0.2–19.6	Yearly average for 1976 (daily averages for 1977–9)
Nanjing	0.094	63	0.11–0.28	Daily averages for 1976
Xuzhou	0.150	47	1.26	Average for the heating periods, 1975–8
Fushun	0.05–0.11	48–63	0.96–2.5	Daily averages for 1974
Standards:				
China	0.150	6–8	0.150	Long-term exposure (daily average)
FRG	0.140	10.5	0.100	Long-term exposure

Source: Kinzelbach (1987: 179).

The consequence of low energy-use efficiency is heavy urban air pollution (Table 5.1). "Pollutant No. 1" is dust. Dustfall and dust quantities exceed environmental standards just about everywhere. Soot and dust are the main sources of polycyclic aromatic hydrocarbons, particularly benzo-apyrene, a highly carcinogenic compound. In Beijing during the heating period, the benzo-apyrene content of the air reaches 6.9g per 100 m^3.

"Pollutant No. 2" is sulphur dioxide. SO_2 concentration in the air exceeds emission standards in several cities. Air pollution poses a severe health hazard in China, responsible for such ailments as lung cancer, cardiovascular disease, chronic bronchitis and chronic nose and ear infections mainly in northern Chinese cities, and silicosis in mining areas. Any comparison between China and Western countries regarding air quality in urban centres is bound to prove unfavourable to China (Kinzelbach 1987: 178–9).

The rural sector

REFORM OF THE AGRICULTURAL SYSTEM

The first reform measures taken in rural areas in 1978 were designed to introduce the principle of direct economic responsibility, that is to loosen administrative controls in agricultural production, enlarge private plots, encourage household sideline production and increase the sale of household products as cash crops on the rural market. Prices of farm inputs were reduced; the prices paid by the state for grain and other agricultural products were increased. Diversification in crop production replaced the costly policy of promoting "grain as the key link", which, for example, had resulted in rice production in highly unfavourable locations. Production incentives were provided by the "household responsibility system", with the family replacing the collective production unit as the key element (responsible for profit and loss) in the agricultural production scheme.

Under the new system, households entered into special agreements with the local collectives, the actual landowners, whereby they contracted to cultivate a certain piece of land, work a forest or raise livestock for the collective. Under these agreements, households were required to meet a procurement quota, and pay an agricultural tax and a fee to the collective. In return, households were permitted to keep agricultural surpluses that they could then sell freely in rural or town markets at prices higher than state prices. The state, in turn, could use its stocks to regulate supply and demand. Falling prices, for instance, could stimulate a change in production patterns.

The basic idea underlying this policy was to transform China's backward system of planned agricultural production into a modern commercial commodity economy. This included subcontracting land and even hiring labour, which, it was hoped, would solve the problem of disguised rural underemployment and unemployment actually affecting millions of people. The result was a boost in production rates; grain output increased from 283 million tonnes in 1977 to 407 million tonnes in 1984. Oil-seed production doubled during that period; cotton production increased by a factor of four. Annual average per capita incomes for farmers increased from 134 yuan in 1978 to 355 yuan in 1984 (Hagemann & Pestel 1987: 162–6).

The revival of the family as the basic production unit, the tremendous increases in agricultural output and the enormous increase in inputs such as agrochemicals have led to several problems: a sharp rise in the rural birthrate, which, despite recent efforts to curb population growth, implies the need for increased food production and more jobs; regional disparity and inequitable distribution of capital inputs; and serious ecological impacts resulting from widespread application of seed–fertilizer technology. Moreover, it appears as though the combined problems can only be solved through the application of traditional agricultural technologies that are capable of reducing waste and increasing the resilience of human ecological cycles, are financially feasible, are sufficiently productive, and can be maintained by the rural population (Hagemann & Pestel 1987: 168) – in short, through the application of ecodevelopment technologies. This assumption leads to two central questions: Is such an ecodevelopment programme possible? What has been the rural policy in China up to now?

For nearly 2000 years, Chinese farmers have practised highly sophisticated, intensive agriculture, including the efficient use of water and irrigation, plant and animal recycling systems, composting, biological and mechanical pest control, waste management and faeces recycling (King 1911). But despite the traditional know-how and modern agricultural inputs, serious ecological damage persists in China. Forests decline despite afforestation programmes; fertile land continues to deteriorate as a result of poor water management, salinization and overfertilizing; karstic landscapes develop. These problems have apparently been aggravated by the contract-farming system. It should be asked, therefore, what environmental policies have contributed to solving these problems, particularly in the fields of water management, forest management, pest management and biogas production.

WATER MANAGEMENT

In the north and northwestern parts of China, most of the underground water resources have been tapped. In the south, irrigation facilities have been installed nearly everywhere and more than half of these are mechanized or power driven. On a national scale, 43 per cent of the total arable land area is irrigated. This implies that a further expansion of the irrigation programme will progress at a much slower rate than it has up to now.

Present efforts in agricultural development and environmental protection include land improvement and better drainage to avoid salinization.

FOREST MANAGEMENT

Only about 12 per cent of the total land area in China is covered by forest. As a consequence, firewood, the most important fuel in rural areas, is scarce. The forested area of Yunnan, a major reserve, declined by 13 per cent over a period of ten years. Forests in Sichuan have declined by as much as 30 per cent since the 1950s. Deforestation in mountainous regions has led to increased severe soil erosion. The Yangzi River is turning murky yellow from the mud of washed-away topsoil. For centuries, the Yellow River has been transporting huge quantities of topsoil eroded away by water. The loss of top-soil implies a general deterioration of agriculture because this loss cannot be compensated by increased applications of fertilizers (Betke 1983: 255–61; Kinzelbach 1987: 180).

Afforestation and reforestation programmes have been the pet policies of successive Chinese leaderships since independence. The plans are to increase forested area by 20 per cent (66 million ha of new forest) by the year 2000. The regions of special attention are northeastern China, Inner Mongolia, Sichuan and Yunnan in the southwest. Combined, these areas contain 50 per cent of the total forested area in China and 60 per cent of the timber reserves. The afforestation programmes are designed to fit into the overall agricultural land-use planning scheme: 40 per cent of the forests should be in mountainous regions, 20 per cent in hilly areas and 10 per cent in the fertile plains.

It is doubtful, however, whether such ambitious plans will come to fruition. The original plans of 1978 – forest had been handed over to private use and responsibility – had to be modified significantly; that is, the programmes had to be cut back by 1979–80. The growing rural population required more arable land and firewood than was compatible with the original afforestation plans. It has since been reported that even local authorities no longer observe all the environmental protection regulations (Betke 1983: 277–94; Hill 1994).

PEST MANAGEMENT

In the late 1970s, Western agricultural delegations to the People's Republic discovered that agricultural practice in China included an advanced form of pest control, namely, integrated pest management (IPM). IPM uses a combination of various biological, chemical and physical techniques in conjunction with traditional farming practices. In a broader sense, plant breeding, cultivation techniques and crop rotation are integral parts of the IPM system.

Between 1949 and 1958, traditional agriculture was practised in China with virtually no developed programme of pest control. DDT was in use, but only to control insects directly harmful to humans. From 1958 to 1970, chemical pesticides dominated the agricultural pest control scene; they were in widespread use particularly on collective farms. Although new varieties of rice had been introduced in China after 1970 to boost rice production, the widespread use of chemical pesticides had eliminated the natural enemies of the plant hopper (an extremely destructive pest) and rice production fell into a crisis between 1970 and 1972. Similar problems occurred with cotton-growing and, as a result, economic and ecological arguments combined in a truly ecodevelopmental effort to search for alternative approaches to pest control.

In 1979, IPM in China was applied over the largest area of any country in the world. Biological control techniques such as the breeding of *Trichogramma* or *Bacillus thuringiensis* were leading in the international agricultural scene, but the concept of agricultural modernization with its four elements, chemicalization, electrification, irrigation and mechanization had not been abandoned. Although IPM and modernization co-exist, the return to family contract-farming is gradually eroding the institutional basis for IPM because it can only be effectively applied over large areas. Although it is conceivable that households could apply some of the IPM measures (for example monitoring), little of this has been reported. It may take quite a few years before new forms of IPM can be incorporated into modernized, small-scale farming (Wagner 1987: 128–36).

BIOGAS PRODUCTION AND ENERGY SUPPLY
Biogas plays only a minute role as a source of energy in China: estimates suggest 1.6 million tonnes hard coal equivalent (hce) per annum or only 1.9 per cent of China's total energy supply. Chinese authorities, however, including the Ministry of Agriculture, rate biogas very highly as a source of rural energy and a valuable substitute for straw, coal and firewood, which thus contributes to the protection of forests and other environmental goals. Following a few isolated attempts before 1949 to establish biogas, it was re-introduced in 1957 by the former Soviet Union and German Democratic Republic. Chinese digester designs transformed the foreign models into smaller-scale facilities, reducing digester capacity from $1000 m^3$ for state farms to between $10m^3$ and $300 m^3$ to supply electricity for villages. After several failures, biogas digesters were finally developed for individual households and put to use successfully, particularly in Sichuan Province, long before household responsibility became part of the politico-economic reform movement. This was a daring political concept at the time, particularly when the Chinese press was attacking rural households as being the main breeding grounds of malcontent and "capitalist ideas".

In 1978, the existence of seven million biogas digesters was reported. Of these, five million were located in Sichuan. A strategy to popularize biogas followed, the goals being 70 per cent of households within a rural production unit operating digesters and the establishment of "excrement management teams" responsible for building, repairing and emptying digesters. The biogas campaign was easy to carry through in the south of China, but in the north, where dry agriculture (use of dry manure) is practised, it met with passive resistance. In spite of its achievements, however, the future of biogas in

100

China in light of the new agricultural policies is uncertain. According to some reports, funds are drying up even for successful waste management teams. According to other reports, new high-quality digesters, requiring little or no maintenance and which can be operated by rural households without technical assistance, will be produced industrially (Wagner 1987: 137–41).

The extensive use of biogas has important implications for economic, energy and environmental policy. The promotion and development of biogas can thus be termed an ecodevelopment measure. Its use as a rural-based energy source would absorb the "excess" rural labour force, and as a substitute for coal it would alleviate pressure on the transport system and contribute to rural self-reliance. Biogas would also be an important substitute for coal and straw (as of 1978, straw was the most widely used rural fuel, exhausted at a rate of 450 million tonnes per year), because straw and coal would be more efficiently employed as industrial resources than as fuels for rural cooking stoves. Biogas could also contribute to maintaining forest reserves as a replacement for firewood. In addition, this would save rural householders 15 working days per year, the total average time needed to cut and gather firewood. According to a 1979 report by the Subgroup for Biological Energies (part of the Special Group for New Energies of the State Science Commission), 70 million households, nearly half of the rural population, suffer from a severe fuel shortage (Wagner 1987: 139). Finally, because biogas sludge and residues are rich in nitrogen, they could be usefully employed as fertilizer to help improve the quality of soil and boost crop production. This has, in fact, been demonstrated successfully in China already.

Environmental policy in the 1990s

In 1990, Qu Geping, director of the National Environmental Protection Agency and deputy chairman of the State Council Environmental Protection Commission, presented China's environmental policy for the following decade (Qu 1990: 103–8; Qu 1991; Qu 1994: 11–14). In his analysis of the problems existing in China, Qu differentiates between pollution due to industrial growth and pollution resulting from stagnation and underdevelopment. In his opinion any environmental policy must begin with environmental management, the decisive factor being that economic development must be strengthened, but also co-ordinated with cost-efficient measures to protect the environment. These would include improving technology at plant level and giving greater power to the bodies concerned with environmental protection in government, ministries and enterprises.

The three components that constitute the backbone of Chinese environmental policy are reminiscent of the political principles adhered to in Germany (see Chapter 4, introduction):

- prevention first (principle of precaution)

- the polluter cleans up (principle of causation: polluter pays)
- increased supervision and management by the state (a modified version of the principle of co-operation).

A preventive policy implies that environmental protection measures must be included in national development plans. With a view to both prevention and control, the environmental impact of such plans is evaluated prior to implementation.

The principle of responsibility functions through the incentive of financial liability in all economic sectors. The following aspects are particularly significant in this regard: the promotion of technological advance, measures for rectification within certain time limits and comprehensive sanitation in urban environments.

Control by the state incorporates a system of financial penalties that are in turn allocated to environmental protection and constitute one-third of the budget for the environment. A multifarious approach is advocated: environmental laws, norms and standards will make up the legislatory basis for management; management and supervisory bodies are to be established at all administrative levels, i.e. central government, provincial, regional and communal; propaganda – education would probably be the preferred term in the West – is to increase environmental awareness among the population.

Concrete measures for the implementation of environmental policy target both national and international goals. Domestic measures emphasize the framework of economic reform and a market economy approach. They include a liability scheme, which includes rewards and penalties, regular evaluation of urban sanitation measures in 32 key cities, and centralized control of air, water and solid waste. Western readers may be astonished that the abolition of all forms of decentralization is advocated so strongly.

At the international and diplomatic level, China's offer of global co-operation in the sphere of environmental protection is particularly significant. Specifically, air and climate problems (which ignore territorial borders) resulting from acid rain, damage to the ozone layer and the greenhouse effect are under discussion here. However, given this kind of co-operation, China reasons that the developed countries – as those mainly responsible for the above problems – would have to considerably increase their efforts towards finding a solution. At the same time, however, China too, as a country that encompasses a vast area, wants to contribute to global protection through domestic measures and, moreover, to participate "enthusiastically" in international initiatives.

In evaluating the programme it should be mentioned that, although interesting political approaches are presented, all in all there is a lack of facts and data and especially very little concrete detail on implementation. The proposals emphasize individual responsibility alongside state control. Both hardly affect the development budget and thus the strategy for economic growth. Cost-extensive environmental policy therefore suits China's economic possibilities and requirements. It is probably fair to say that it is these relationships that are being described in China as a co-ordination of ecology and economy. Thus, in its rhetoric, Chinese environmental policy has also moved away from an ecological towards an economical approach.[1]

5.3 Population and culture

Population development and policy

Almost 23 per cent of the world's population lives in China; by the year 2000 the absolute figure for China's population is expected to exceed 1200 million. Population development is affected by the availability of natural resources, especially arable land, and in turn influences the overall economic and ecological situation.

Population policy first became an issue in China in 1962, after the failure of the Great Leap Forward had led to severe famines and mass unemployment. Family planning and the two-child family were propagated until the Cultural Revolution was initiated in 1966. It was only after the Mao Zedong era in 1978-9 that the present strict one-child family campaign was announced and family planning became a constitutional duty. Administrative and social pressure, and economic incentives and penalties were used to set and meet targets (World Bank 1981, Annex B: 83-9; Aird 1990, Jowett 1990). The measures are not popular among the population, so it is not easy to assess the future of Chinese population policy.

Population development in the past is equally difficult to evaluate because the available statistics are often either incomplete or unreliable; experts are thus forced to do their own calculations on the basis of limited data, as is also the case in the following overview (cf. Scharping 1989: 34–47; for the historical perspective, cf. Hu & Zou 1991: 1–28).

China's population has doubled between 1949 (541 million) and 1987 (1080 million). A total of 94 per cent of the Chinese live in the fertile East,

1. Lester Ross views the future of Chinese environmental policy sceptically (Ross 1988: 210). On the other hand, sectors of the scientific establishment (not free of political influence) are becoming more concerned with environmental issues. Within the Chinese Academy of Sciences these are, for example, the National Conditions Investigation Group (Wang 1992), and especially the Research Center for Eco-Environmental Sciences (RCEES), which has 539 employees(RCEES 1992) and includes the Department of Systems Ecology, whose portfolio ranges from human ecosystems to applications in urban and regional planning (Wang et al. 1990, Wang et al. 1991, Hu & Wang 1991). The University of Agriculture in Beijing has held international conferences on environmental issues: in 1985 on salinization, and in 1993 on resource management and sustainable agriculture. The concept of ecological land use is thus gaining in importance (Cheng Xu et al. 1992, Ministry of Agriculture 1992)

the traditional homeland of Chinese culture, where the population density ranges up to 2000 persons per km² of arable land. The urbanization rate has grown steadily – a consequence of the successful hygiene campaigns in the cities; the urban population grew from 10 per cent in 1949 to 16 per cent in 1958, shot up to 19 per cent during the Great Leap, due to the industrialization campaign, and levelled off at around 17 per cent, following the anti-urban policy in the 1960s and 1970s. With the beginning of the economic reforms in 1978, a massive flow of population to the cities started. The urbanization rate increased from 19 per cent in 1979 to 36 per cent in 1985, and may reach 50 per cent by 2000. A major cause of migration to the cities was hidden rural unemployment or underemployment that became manifest after the dissolution of the people's communes (Chan & Xu 1985: 583–613; Scharping 1989:39–41; Jowett 1990: 125; Tang & Jenkins 1990: 204–18).

According to *China's Agenda 21*, and official document and "White Paper" dealing with the issues of sustainability as they relate to China's population, environment and development in the twenty-first century, every effort will be made:

> . . . to keep the average annual rate of population growth within 1.25 per cent by the year 2000. The total birth rate will be reduced from 2.3 in 1990 to below 2.0, the average birth rate in developed countries at present. It is expected that the Chinese population will be stabilized at around 1.5 or 1.6 billion [thousand million] by the middle of next century. The population policy includes genetic counselling, childbirth counselling, and education about child-rearing practices with the aim of improving general health and educational levels. (Anon. 1994: 51)

Between 100 and 270 million people will be seeking employment by the end of the century. The crucial question is whether China will be able – as planned – to channel some of the labour force into smaller towns, or whether the huge conurbations will grow larger and as a result produce all the detrimental environmental impacts discussed earlier. The second question is whether China will succeed in reducing the fertility rate further. Those born during the years of high birth rates that followed the Great Leap have been reaching their legal marriage age since 1985, and many would prefer two children to a one-child family.

Calculations by the Natural Resources Comprehensive Survey Committee of the Chinese Academy of Sciences suggest that available agricultural resources are capable of supporting 1500 million people, if calculated to the minimum standard. The figure for an environmentally compatible population may be even smaller, depending on natural restrictions such as non-renewable resources or absorption capacities. Given total fertility rates of between 1.9 and 2.2, the total population will be 1300–1600 million in 2050 and 1000–1700 million in 2100 (Hu & Zou 1991: 203–4).

Cultural tradition

Consistency in China's environmental policy despite political changes can be traced in part to the Chinese heritage. It was in fact not so very long ago that the Chinese society was an agrarian society completely dependent upon natural recycling, the re-use of agricultural wastes, the use of organic manure fertilizers, biological pest control, multi-cropping and low energy inputs – in short, what can be called "ecofarming" techniques. This approach to agriculture was, to some extent, transferred to industrial production.

Another attempt to explain China's consistency in environmental policy maintains that dialectical materialism was already deeply rooted in Chinese thought and attitudes. The notion of "walking on two legs" means that two opposing or apparently contradictory approaches are just two sides of the same coin. Differing approaches may eventually be combined but, in any case, each may stand in its own right. In matters of agricultural production, for instance, this attitude still pervades the thought of Chinese planners; it ensures any one of two ways is never really completely eliminated.

This kind of thinking has its roots in Taoism, whereas the pervasive benevolent Chinese attitude towards nature is inherent in Buddhist ideas. But how to explain "un-Taoist action contrary to nature" (Tuan 1968, cited in Callicott & Ames 1989: 283) such as the construction of the Chinese Wall, massive deforestation and, more recently, devastating air and water pollution? Tuan believes that the Chinese are alternately under either yin or yang influence. During yin periods human innovations are adapted to prevailing natural conditions in accordance with the principles of feng-shui geomancy. This is described as the art of "taking proper note of the forms of hills, and directions of water courses since these are themselves the outcome of the moulding influences of winds and waters" (Callicott & Ames 1989: 284; see also Fig. 1.20 in this volume). During yang periods the "masculine" heavenly principle dominates the "feminine" earthly principle, so that the Earth itself is subjected to gross disregard and blatant exploitation. According to this view, the Mao Zedong (Mao Tse-Tung) years would constitute a yang period, whereas present efforts to prevent and control environmental degradation in China could count as evidence for a yin ascendancy.

Some authors (Yu 1987b) maintain that a major factor behind Mao's political success was the adaptation of Marxism, in the sense that Chinese philosophy – including its practical bent – was reconstructed for evolutionary purposes. Thus Mao's interpretation of the classical Confucianist debate on the relationship between knowledge (zhi) and practice (xing) was in accordance with the neo-Confucianist philosopher Wang Yangming (1472–1528) in that it emphasized the unity between the two: "To discover truth (knowing) through practice (doing), and through practice to verify and develop truth" (Mao 1965: 308, cited in Yu 1987b: 27). This interpretation relates to less common Western traditions concerning theory and practice. One

105

manifestation is discussed elsewhere in this volume: the relationship between cognition and production. Cognition and production are seen to be identical in structure: "productive" exploitation of nature presupposes the "theory of exploitation" in science, technology and economics (cf. §1.2 and §8.3).

5.4 Conclusion

While China had appalling pollution problems from the beginning of the Mao Zedong era, there were also attempts made as early as this to alleviate some of the difficulties. Many of the efforts targeted the health of the affected population, but also had an environmental impact. However, the Stockholm Conference in 1972 seems to mark the turning point where environmental considerations were afforded greater attention than previously.

The United Nations Environment Programme and its ideals were the catalyst behind China's more recent environmental policy programme. China's development approach was an ecodevelopment approach, whether intentionally or accidentally, because it held to the conviction that environmental considerations were an integral part of development policy and, ultimately, economic and ecological issues could not be reasonably separated. This conviction was very obvious in China's rural development policy, as well illustrated by the integrated pest management programme, energy policy and biogas development. It was less obvious in Chinese urban industrial policy, in whose earlier stages strategies such as waste recycling and energy saving were strongly promoted only for economic reasons. As public health deteriorated and working conditions steadily worsened, and as environmental hazards and the effects of environmental damage in rural and urban settings made themselves felt, it became clear to the Chinese leadership that neglect of these factors also had serious implications.

On the other hand, environmental policy in China was never fully or completely successfully implemented, despite its serious intention, consistency and bureaucratic support. Several factors can be attributed to its shortcomings. China, a developing country as large as Europe, made some specific achievements in environmental policy, but it simply lacks the financial resources to install expensive technology on a large scale. There was little incentive at factory level to implement cost-intensive policies. There was little enforcement of policy through fines by state authorities, because this would imply the state *qua* property owner taking money out of one pocket and putting it in another (robbing Peter to pay Paul). Bureaucracies are usually not made to implement novel strategies. Successive failures of economic reforms suggest that not much more can be expected of environmental policy. A well-planned and sophisticated environmental protection policy is useless if, at the same time, economic reform abolishes the very institutions needed to implement policy measures (e.g. China's IPM programme and, to some extent, the biogas programme were dependent upon the collectives, but these institutions were abolished by agro-economic reform). Such counter-productive effects will have to be eliminated if Chinese environmental policy in its ecodevelopment approach is to be successfully implemented.

The worry, though, is that one can only look after the environment if one is rich enough, whereas most evidence suggests that wealth in fact causes environmental degradation, which is often enough exported to poorer areas. This issue is crucial to China, as it is to Europe. Does China still have the scope, as a "developing country" to develop into an ecologically sound society? If fundamental changes are too late for Europe, are they perhaps feasible in a country that is changing rapidly and can look back upon an environmentally benign tradition in its cultural history?

CHAPTER 6
A human ecology approach to sustainable agricultural development: the Andaman and Nicobar Islands

In 1986 the Indian islands of Andaman and Nicobar, which are located in the Bay of Bengal, were visited by their Prime Minister, Rajiv Gandhi. He could not discern any development activities on the islands and asked why this was the case. His question provoked enormous activity, most significantly, perhaps, an expert seminar held in Port Blair in 1987 to which I was also invited. The object of the seminar was to draw up a set of political options for development and environmental planning on the islands. The (mostly Indian) participants were divided over the question as to whether this group of islands should be left in peaceful and happy complacency or whether they should be awakened from their slumber and guided into twentieth and twenty-first century reality, so that they could in turn contribute to the development of the Indian mainland. The line was drawn between economically orientated developers and more ecologically minded conservationists, whereby the local experts, scientists and administrators living in Port Blair, clearly favoured conservationist views, preferring to keep outside influence to a minimum. There were no tribal representatives present. It was interesting to observe that the conservationist view gained more influence as the week-long seminar progressed.

Here, some of the proposals for development are outlined and their social and ecological consequences evaluated. Then a set of recommendations, which could act as a rough guideline for an ecodevelopment approach, are presented. They may not only be of regional value, but also serve as a paradigm for any development that adheres to the principles of human ecology. This view is a personal one and steers a course somewhere between the two extremes of massive development and non-development. Finally, the present political reality on the Andaman and Nicobar Islands is described.

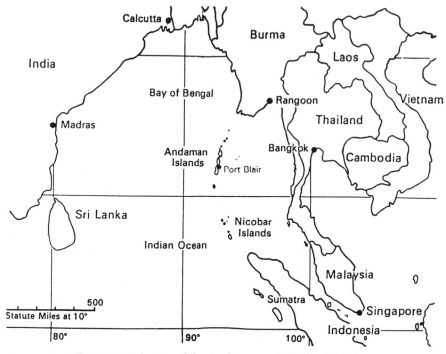

Figure 6.1 Location of the Andaman and Nicobar Islands.

6.1 A case study for sustainable development policy

An example of a holistic and sustainable development policy based on human ecology can be demonstrated by the situation on the Andaman and Nicobar Islands. The suggestions developed below represent a step in the direction of policy-orientated counselling; as such they target application and implementation.

Database

Information on the Andaman and Nicobar Islands has been sketchy and obscure, and the database limited. The first information recorded on these islands came from Claudius Ptolemaeus, the great Roman geographer, who lived in Alexandria in the second century. Ptolemaeus, who had never seen Andaman or Nicobar, described the islands as "Islands of the Cannibals". The next reference to these islands is found in the writings of I'Tsing, a Chinese traveller who arrived in India in AD 673. He referred to the islands

110

as "Andaban" and also described their inhabitants, evidently on the basis of hearsay, as cannibals. Marco Polo, the famous Venetian traveller, journeyed near the islands around 1260. He described the inhabitants like this: "All the men of this island have heads like dogs, and teeth and eyes like dogs; for I assure you that the whole aspect of their faces is that of big mastiffs" (Singh 1978: 1–2).

Despite these obvious historical inaccuracies, there is nevertheless abundant written information on these islands. There is also much expertise to be drawn upon in Port Blair itself, and there is in fact a small, but accurate, first-hand empirical database to supplement the previous ones, that is observational impressions. Port Blair was founded by the British as a penal colony for their Indian colonial empire. During the Second World War, the islands were occupied by the Japanese. They passed to independent India in 1947 as a centrally administered union territory with limited sovereignty.

The Andaman and Nicobar Islands are located 1200 km east of the Indian subcontinent and are the remains of a former land bridge that extended from Burma to Sumatra. They extend between 6° and 13° on the northern parallel, thus falling in the tropical rain zone with 200 days of precipitation per annum. Dense tropical rain forests are the dominant form of vegetation on these almost unspoiled islands. Along the coast, they are encircled by mangrove forests. Coral banks in shallow sea stretch out in front of white, sandy beaches. The entire area encompasses 8300 km^2.

Most of the approximately 550 islands are uninhabited. The Indian census estimates the number of inhabitants in 1981 at 190 000, up from 50 000 in 1971. Of these, 22 000 are negroid descendants of the island's original inhabitants, and Asian immigrants of a tribal character, some of whom continue to live in complete isolation from civilization. The rest of the population consists of the so-called locals, descendants of the Indian prisoners in and around Port Blair, as well as Indian immigrants and administrators from the mainland who have formed the political and economic elite since 1947.

Twenty per cent of the population is engaged in agricultural production. The chief crops grown on the 48 000 ha of cultivated land are rice and vegetables, followed by coconut and fruit trees. Tropical wood is processed in saw mills: in 1984 this amounted to 182 000 m^3. Despite the existence of a plenitude of sea life, the fishing industry has hardly developed. Except for the saw mills, there is no industrial production.

Some political proposals and their supposed social and ecological impacts

Before I visited Port Blair, the capital of the Andaman and Nicobar Islands, in 1987, I tried to sort out those political proposals that could have major

111

impacts on the future development of the islands. The basis of most of my information consisted of rumours, newspaper articles, and information gathered from consultations with experts. According to these sources, three major development proposals could be identified:

- a proposal for a defence area to test missiles,
- a proposal for a tourist centre,
- a proposal for a free-trade zone including a duty-free port.

MISSILE TESTING SITE

According to *India Today* (Ahmed 1987: 62–3), the Defence Ministry had been trying for the past four years to set up a National Test Range (NTR) in Orissa, Balasore District (estimated cost: Rs30000 million). Because of extremely strong opposition from local inhabitants it was suggested that the NTR be located in the Andaman Islands where fewer individuals would be affected – and possibly where opposition would not be so strong.

There are defence and budgetary arguments both for and against the Andaman Islands as a testing site, but more relevant to my purposes is a consideration of why the Orissa population resisted so strongly, because the reasons may prove valid for the Andamans as well. For the Orissa farmers, "the area, spread over 400km^2 along the seashore and comprising 132 villages, is a virtual gold-mine with cash crops like betel-vines, coconuts and cashew besides profitable fishing in the shallow waters . . ." (Ahmed 1987: 63). Local farmers claimed that the NTR project would destroy vast paddy fields, 30000 betel-vines, thousands of coconut palms and cashew plants at a value of over Rs1750 million. Thus, the planned resettlement of farmers and their families could not only bring about the destruction of an ecosystem, it could also destroy a human ecological system where societal groups live in harmony with nature. This same argument could, of course, be applied to the Andaman or the Nicobar Islands should the NTR be located there.

TOURIST CENTRE

What is tourism? A tourist was previously understood to be a person who was curious about the nature and lifestyles of other persons in other parts of the world. It was this curiosity that made the tourist travel. Because of this simple definition, we sometimes still believe that tourism promotes understanding between peoples. Today, however, the tourist has been degraded into a foreign-exchange-carrying animal from whom local inhabitants or governments attempt to extract as much money as possible. Because tourists are willing to surrender to this exploitation, they are permitted to retaliate by exploiting the local environment and disrupting local social structures. For example:

- Trekking in Nepal has had severe environmental consequences that threaten traditional Nepalese society.

- Coastal tourism in East Africa led to rising expectations among the local population. Children began to earn much more than their fathers as hard-working fishermen had ever earned; social hierarchies were upturned.
- Sex tourism in Thailand has disrupted local cultural values and beliefs.

What do these examples show? Again, although the impacts may be more subtle than those of the proposed NTR, human ecological systems will be affected. The impacts may be for the better or the worse, so the question should be raised as to how these systems can be affected for the better, that is, how can the greatest damage be avoided? Ghetto tourism, where tourists living in a camp are kept apart from the indigenous population outside, was a partial answer to this, but ghetto tourism seems to be on the decline. According to Willibald Pahr, Secretary General of the World Tourism Organisation (WTO), experiences with ghetto tourism have not been favourable (Koth 1987: 19).

Another answer to this problem was given by countries like China, Burma and Tanzania. To cite one example, Gertrude Mongella, Minister of Tourism in Tanzania, stated that her country was opposed to mass tourism and, consequently, sex tourism does not play a role. Tanzania's tourist policy is to make the country attractive for educated persons who show a specific interest for the local countryside and local culture (ibid.: 19).

Interestingly, the Tanzanian tourist policy led back to the original definition of a tourist, which was thought to be obsolete – a person who is curious about other people. It is also worth noting that this concept of tourism had an elitist element to it. Moreover, this elitist way of thinking was being propagated by socialist countries – an amazing switch of values! My question is, therefore: is elitist behaviour necessary to protect human ecological systems, that is, to protect social systems and their natural environments?

FREE-TRADE ZONE AND PORT

For years, there has been talk of making Great Nicobar a duty-free port. Hong Kong's future remains uncertain, Singapore is crowded, and Great Nicobar is situated on the trade routes between India, Burma, Southeast Asia and the Far East. What role does Hong Kong play in this? It could either serve as a model for Great Nicobar or it could provide the needed capital for development as a result of its own political and economic uncertainty.

It is not likely that Hong Kong will provide the source of capital for Great Nicobar. First, those Chinese who were able and willing to leave the crown colony have already done so and made new homesteads in the Caribbean. Secondly, Hong Kong is flowering economically at present. Thirdly, and most importantly, there is no ethnic Chinese minority on the Andaman or the Nicobar Islands. There is a strong Hindustani-speaking tradition on these islands, so the chances are better that they will attract floating Indian capital, including that of Hong Kong Indians who will lose their national identity in

1997 when the crown colony becomes part of the People's Republic of China.

There are many possible objections to the proposed free-trade zone, but one is particularly significant. On the Nicobar Islands, there is still a growing aboriginal population. These islands are one of the few areas in the world that are almost untouched, with a functioning human ecological system virtually free from outside influences. For this reason, the Indian Anthropological Survey protested against the institution of a free-trade port. Whether, as Iqbal Singh (1978: 305) suggests, it would be possible to make Great Nicobar a duty-free port but leave the other islands untouched, is still an open question.

Preliminary conclusion

It is not my opinion that all efforts to develop the Andaman and Nicobar Islands are *a priori* wrong. However, I do believe that those responsible must be extremely careful. There is no government in the world that can easily afford to destroy human ecological systems. Any recommendation should take this into account. The costs and benefits of development must also be calculated, but not in purely monetary terms. What would be the price, for example, of the Nicobarese human ecological systems, which, once they are destroyed, cannot be rehabilitated. Finally, it will be necessary to differentiate between who will share the benefits and who will bear the costs of development.

6.2 Three models for future development

The following recommendations represent an attempt to present some ideas – following the concept of holistic human ecology – concerning the future prospects of the islands, albeit based on limited observational data. This includes possible benefits to their inhabitants. I shall therefore proceed with a good deal of caution.

As a result of the information collected, three basic models of future development (Fig. 6.2) would seem to apply to the Andaman and the Nicobar Islands:

- an ecological preservation/social stagnation model
- a macropolis model, and
- an ecodevelopment model.

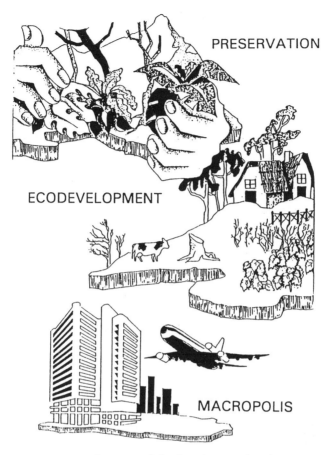

Figure 6.2 Three models for future development.
Source: Glaeser (1989b).

Ecological preservation and social stagnation

These islands represent one of the very few, perhaps the only, specimens of truly natural ecosystems that have hardly been influenced anthropogenically. It is argued, therefore, that these islands must be preserved as they are. This has consequences for the three population groups on the islands, the tribals, including an aboriginal population, the so-called "locals" and recent immigrants, including government and administrative officials. Some islands are populated with aborigines who live in harmony with their island environment. In view of the present slaughtering of Amazonian peoples, the aboriginal inhabitants of the Andamans and Nicobars may soon become the

115

last undisturbed autochthonous communities on Earth and, as such, their lives, lifestyles, culture and environment ought to be preserved.

To achieve this, outside influence should be kept to a minimum, but this can only be realized if "civilized" humans are not permitted to disturb the aborigines. The "locals" should be confined to Port Blair and a few "civilized" peripheral spots. This implies that no further colonization of the islands will be permitted and that immigration is ruled out. It further implies social stagnation in order to preserve an original human culture. It is obvious that this model cannot tolerate development that would include military ventures, capital- and technology-intensive endeavours like a free-trade zone, or any significant form of tourism.

Macropolis

This model would make a new Hong Kong of Great Nicobar. A possible five million people living on some $860 \, km^2$ would result in a population density of 5800 per km^2. In view of this figure, it would not be too far-fetched to say that more islands would be needed, be they for reasons of pleasure or for agricultural supply; such a development creates its own dynamics. According to the proponents of this model, the development would be desirable because of its expected pull effect on the mainland economy. The anticipated economic benefits would outweigh the social costs of development that – in "extrapolating" the present scenario – could include the following: the "locals" will lose their cultural identity; the Shompen, the tribals on Great Nicobar, will disappear; the Nicobarese will decay and their numbers will dwindle. The economic benefits, it is argued, would also outweigh the ecological destruction suffered by Great Nicobar and the other islands. To the contrary, it is argued that human welfare is more important than nature protection, and that the economic and social benefits of the macropolis model will reach the locals and Nicobarese through the trickle-down mechanism, once these peoples have been "civilized".

Ecodevelopment

The ecodevelopment model is located between the extremes. Ecodevelopment has two roots: ecology and development (cf. §2.3). Therefore the *contradiction* between development or growth and environment becomes the *dialectics* of development plus environment. It implies that accelerated economic development be, at the same time, ecologically and socially sound or at least benign.

Ecodevelopment policy (cf. Glaeser 1984: 9–12) begins by considering the needs of the people. Thus, the elimination of poverty is a precondition of

116

economic development, not its result. Similarly, the priority no longer lies in export earnings, but in creating employment in the domestic economy and in enhancing a broad income distribution. Employment includes self-employment at the monetary as well as at the subsistence level.

The planning of ecodevelopment projects is shaped by several factors. First, the sociocultural values and behavioural patterns of the peasant family, and the politico-administrative scope of the village community are major determinants. Secondly, the economic limitations, in terms of low-income earners who may be partially embedded in a subsistence economy, are also important. Finally, the biophysical environment may impose natural constraints. Selecting an appropriate location for a project is governed by the ability of those responsible for the planning process to harmonize socio-cultural, economic and ecological factors, which may require democratic resolution of social conflicts.

How does this concept translate into action for the Andaman and the Nicobar Islands? Let us consider the answer to this query in terms of the three elements, needs, self-reliance and environmental compatibility.

NEEDS ORIENTATION AND PARTICIPATION

The islanders involved, the "beneficiaries" of new development measures, would be asked about their desires and wishes. The optimal form of partici-pation would be for them to take active part in the planning process. Active participation is preceded by an adequate information policy that is designed to create awareness among the inhabitants, who comprise "locals" and other residents. The decision as to whether "locals" should be granted special minority rights is a political one. The tribals are not addressed because it is assumed that any measure that affects them would be harmful.

SELF-RELIANCE

It will be most important to strengthen the major economic sector, agricul-ture, because this is the only means to stabilize the island economy. The agri-cultural decline after Japanese occupation has led to the islands' further dependency on the mainland. The islands enjoy a tropical climate with annual rainfalls of 325 mm in the southeast, more than 325 mm in the south-west, and 150 mm in the north. Under these tropical conditions rice is the staple crop along with pulses, oil-seeds, sugar cane, sweet potato and other vegetables, and fruits such as papayas, pineapples, mangoes, oranges and bananas. Plantation crops include coconut, tea, coffee and rubber. From the point of view of self-reliance (but also for ecological reasons), food crops, especially subsistence crops, must be favoured over plantation crops for export.

Rice can be cultivated at varying altitudes from sea level up to 1600 m. In South Andaman, rice is grown chiefly in valleys and on the coastal plains, but also in scattered plots on hills and slopes. Because of the abundant rainfall, irrigation is not necessary. Rice cultivation is sometimes alternated with cultivation of vegetables, as is so often done in the tropics. Rice is sown from June to August and harvested from October to December. Vegetables are cultivated between January and March. This system, which is climatically and economically appropriate, can probably be improved upon, intensified, and even expanded without causing any harm. It could also be supplemented with additional crops such as cassava (known as the "famine crop" in East Africa), other vegetables and spices(e.g. pepper) which can also be used as cash crops, and with crops such as beans and soybeans.

In terms of agriculture and fisheries, some small-scale processing industries could be built up, so that manufacturing surpluses and increased employment would further benefit the islands. These industries could be centred around rice husks (for cement production), the coconut (for oil, charcoal, fibres, etc.), and vegetables, fruits and fish (for canning). Rural energy needs could, to some extent, be satisfied through animal husbandry with biogas units, or with solar power. A system of rainwater collectors and reservoirs would be useful for irrigation in the dry season, mainly on non-rice-growing hillslopes.

ENVIRONMENTAL COMPATIBILITY
It has been claimed that, on the basis of existing agricultural practices, crop production can be intensified, even extended to hillsides, without endangering the ecology of the agricultural system itself, and this means its economic basis. The secret is that the agricultural system, although productive, imitates the natural ecosystem. It is thus an "agro-ecosystem", taking up the dialectics of the combined term "eco-development".

The general strategy of ecofarming (Egger & Martens 1987: 153–5) is based upon the dual aim of conservation and productivity. At least the scattered remnants of the natural landscape with their various biotopes and species should be conserved. On the Andamans and Nicobars, this would consist of tropical rain forest in valleys, on slopes and hilltops, as well as coastal strips of mangrove. In such areas genetic plant material, which may be badly needed later, would be preserved.

Preservation of diversity is also important for cultivated areas. We distinguish between species diversity and biotope diversity, whereby biotope diversity provides the basis for species diversity. Ecological niches can be created by conserving patches of forests and hedges, through intensive fallows, mixed cropping systems, and reduced weeding. Maintaining species diversity includes preserving species that are not directly part of the productive system. This type of conservation safeguards the basic ecological production factors, namely, soil, nutrients, humus, water balance and erosion control. Animals, from birds to soil bacteria, are part of this system.

The four main goals of ecofarming are thus to:
• ensure ecophysicological functions

118

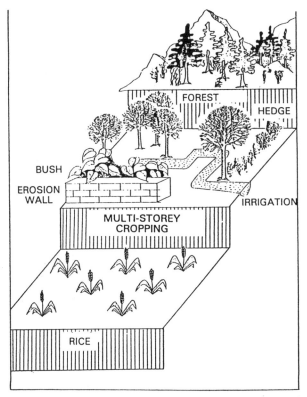

Figure 6.3 An ecodevelopment solution for South Andaman. *Source:* Glaeser (1989b).

- preserve a multiplicity of biotopes
- preserve a high species diversity, and
- create an aesthetically pleasing landscape.

Three important rules of ecofarming accompany these goals:

- give subsistence priority over markets (this is, however, by no means exclusive)
- give long-term harvest security priority over short-term maximization of profits
- use farm and local resources instead of external inputs ("low-input farming").

Once an area such as South Andaman is sufficiently well understood, it would be useful to take the following steps and measures. First, an eco-design for the valleys, hills and slopes must be drawn up. Secondly, the cultivation method must be defined. It would identify environmental dangers such as erosion, pest damage, or loss of soil fertility, and it would suggest measures for regeneration and improved production. Regeneration measures

119

might include, for example, the integration of green manuring and animal husbandry. Productive measures might include, for instance, mixed or multi-storey cropping and crop rotation. Finally, these measures could be supported by additional equipment, especially mechanical devices, or specific agricultural practices such as manure fertilization or integrated pest management.

To turn this general strategy into a package of recommendations for South Andaman, we must appeal to local traditional systems and build upon local knowledge and expertise, which could, however, be improved. One possible solution is shown in Figure 6.3. Paddy is grown in the valleys, alternating with mixed vegetable gardening. On the slopes, multi-storey cropping is practised. This could consist of, for example, neem, mango or other fruit trees; a second layer might contain bananas; on the ground, irrigated or dry vegetable mixed crops, including some legumes, could be cultivated. Each layer could be interspersed with cassava (tapioca). The planting would follow horizontal contour lines to avoid erosion. A few horizontal rows of hedges, bushes or green fodder grasses would have a similar effect. Finally, hilltops would be left undisturbed; the rain forest is to be maintained in order to retain moisture and as a further anti-erosion measure.

SOCIOCULTURAL VIABILITY

The economic and agricultural recommendations are certainly *ecologically* viable, but are they also *socially* compatible and *culturally appropriate*? The tribals would not be affected if they do not wish to be. They would still be able to live in harmony with their natural, physical environment. Their values, beliefs and customs would not be touched.

For the Indian locals, more economic independence and, consequently, more political self-reliance would be a major impact of the proposed measures. Agricultural intensification, small-scale industry, fishing and tourism would produce higher incomes and additional jobs. If such policies were handled carefully, this would not imply that decision-making is controlled by the new immigrants, although there would be this danger. The recommendations build upon local traditions; the immigrants take care of cultural and social change, within the limits of the desired economic development.

Recommendations

The three basic models listed above are those from which policy-makers have to choose: preservation, macropolis, or ecodevelopment.[1] On the basis of the pros and cons of all three models, the following tentative recommendations are made:

- The islands should basically retain their typical characteristics as regards landscape, ecosystem and social settings.

- This does not preclude, on the basis of present amenities, developments and natural wealth, the promotion of carefully planned improvements, which could sustain cautious immigration from the mainland. Forced immigration and the opening up of new settlements or unpopulated islands for the sake of rapid economic growth is not advocated.

The reasons for these general lines of recommendation are manifold. There are distinct economic cost disadvantages due to the long distance of the islands to the mainland (transport costs) and to the lack of infrastructure and skills on the islands. The main capital of the islands, on the other hand, is their scenic beauty and unspoiled landscape. Rapid changes and massive influx from outside would threaten the cultural identity of the local population. Tribals would lose their territory or face changes in their living conditions, as has occurred previously in colonial times, which could eventually lead to their extinction. Finally, the islands represent (or soon will represent) the only untouched natural ecosystem on the globe. The tropical rain forest, once cut down, will not grow back again, because of the poor quality of tropical soils and other factors (not to be confused with the large turnover of biomass suggesting high soil fertility).

From these general lines of recommendation some more specific suggestions can be gleaned:

- Agriculture must be intensified in order to increase the self-sufficiency of the islands. Ecologically orientated methods such as ecofarming or agroforestry should be applied so that the delicate tropical ecological equilibrium can be maintained and, forexample, soil erosion can be avoided. Agricultural measures should centre on food crops such as paddy, vegetables and fruits, rather than plantation and export crops.
- Fishing should be increased in the interest of island self-sufficiency. This would include coastal fishing on a small scale to avoid overfishing.
- Processing industries on the basis of agriculture and small-scale fishing should be introduced to create employment and a momentum of economic acceleration.
- It is recommended that environmentally and socially responsible "soft tourism", attracting individuals fond of the "natural capital" of the islands (their beauty, calmness and unspoiled beaches), be promoted. This would save both monetary capital and natural resources as compared with the facilities needed for conventional mass tourism.
- It is furthermore recommended that facilities be created to attract

---

1. To provide a rational base for choice is an ethical–political necessity, in spite of a certain probability that the macropolis model will ultimately be adopted by vested interests, particularly if oil exploration proves successful. Test-drilling and exploration have already been attempted in some areas. This serves as a further example of how ethical solutions are overridden by other considerations.

middle-class tourists. Domestic and international tourists should mingle. This would require two or three luxury hotels (the existing ones included) of limited size and a few middle-class hotels and lodges in Port Blair. Tourist transportation should include regular air and ship service from Madras, Calcutta, and perhaps Bangkok and Singapore, as well as a fleet of small motorboats and electric glass-bottomed boats for inter-island hopping. Tourist activities should be restricted, more or less, to sightseeing tours, day tours to beaches, and some overnight camping. Tourists who feel they want more than this can find their way easily to Pattaya and Phuket in Thailand (places with which competition is not necessarily desirable).

For reasons already stated, a free port and trading zone is not the recommended development model for the Andaman and the Nicobar Islands. Competition with Hong Kong, Singapore, and possible new sites would be tremendous, particularly in the face of severe comparative locational disadvantages such as no trading and supply hinterland, lack of a basic, stable economic background, lack of infrastructure, including education and skills, and high transport costs.

Moreover, unique ecosystems and tribal societies will not only be endangered; they face unequivocal extinction. This is particularly true for the Shompen who inhabit the high plains of Great Nicobar, the southernmost and largest of the Nicobar islands. Unfortunately, Great Nicobar, owing to its natural port facilities, size, and favourable geographical location is the obvious choice for a free-trade zone.

Finally, for the promotion of "soft tourism" as described above, duty-free wines, as are permitted in the territory of Goa, would be sufficient. In addition, certain limited goods could be offered for sale in duty-free shops, although not on the scale of Hong Kong or Singapore. Such practices would save the major part of the islands, particularly Great Nicobar, from destruction. The consequences of such a solution were described by Sen (1962: 188) as follows: "These tropical islands depict wonderfully the primitive nature of life, subjected to the local geography, experiencing a healthy and peaceful growth."

6.3 The Andaman and Nicobar Islands today

So much for the human-ecology–orientated scenario for development. It would be Utopian to expect an emerging-market economy such as India in a world dominated by Western material values to fully adopt the approach outlined above. However, the principles of preservation and self-reliance, at least for the indigenous population of the island groups, were given much consideration in planning at government level and are now being followed.

On 5 December 1992 I was able to interview Professor Dr Kailash C. Malhotra from the Indian Statistical Institute in Calcutta on this matter. Malhotra co-ordinated an official commission surveying the situation on the Andaman and Nicobar Islands in the light of decisions taken by the central government in Delhi in 1992. This expert commission was set up by the central Ministry of the Environment, the Ministry of Tourism and the local government (Department of Science and Technology) in Port Blair, and was mainly concerned with the tribals and their problems with health and survival. The commission was to meet again for further consultations on how the tribals could be helped.

The basic decision taken by the government in 1992 was to allow Indians and foreigners to travel to Port Blair without need of a special visa and to visit any island except those inhabited by tribals, in particular the Onge, Jarawas, Sentinelese and Greater Andamanese. Scientists are required to obtain special approval from the local administration in order to visit tribal islands. Responsibility for tribals lies with the Department of Social Welfare in Port Blair; the governor has the authority to grant (or deny) permission to prospective visitors. According to Malhotra, initial contact with the Sentinelese was established in January 1990. By December 1992 the Onge language had become familiar to scientists, who are now in the process of learning Jarawa and hope to start with the Sentinelese language soon. At present, even these scientists are not permitted to stay overnight on the tribal islands to study the languages. The explanation given for this restriction is that although there is no problem concerning the social integration of the remaining 28 Greater Andamanese, the 97 Onge suffer from tuberculosis, venereal diseases and a high rate of infant mortality. Whether the extinction of these tribals is still due to a prolonged cultural shock resulting from contact with Indian or Western civilization, or whether the crisis can be reduced to a matter of mere health problems that can be overcome through proper treatment and prevention, as claimed by the expert commission, remains debatable.

There has been no major discussion or activity concerning the environment–ecology issue. In 1992 I found a note in a German newspaper stating that plans for a tourist centre on two of the untouched islands, Middle Andaman and Havelock Island, were under way (*Der Tagesspiegel*, 4 October 1992). Hotel development may now expand to the other islands, including Great Nicobar. At present, both Port Blair and Great Nicobar are connected to the mainland by air. There was some opposition to these decisions by local non-governmental organizations (NGOs) and mainland environmental groups, but the movement was neither large enough nor powerful enough to have any impact on the intentions of the government.

6.4 Conclusion

The object of this chapter was to elucidate possibilities for sustainable agricultural development and to demonstrate how they could be put into effect in an environment largely untarnished by industrialization and the environmental degradation that it usually entails. In devising models for development on the Andaman and Nicobar Islands, an attempt was made to draw upon the holistic human ecology paradigm, in so far as the development approach proposed is autonomous and takes the natural environment and the sociocultural milieus affected into consideration. Unfortunately, political realities do not always comply with model scenarios.

While it is generally easy to see why such extreme measures as military developments are destructive to societies or ecological systems, the question I wish to raise is whether development in general also poses a threat to such systems. The planned resettlement of farmers and their families, for instance, could not only bring about the destruction of an ecosystem, it could also destroy a human ecological system where societal groups live in harmony with nature. There are a good many examples supporting this hypothesis and if we consider the varieties of development envisaged, we must ask ourselves:

- What do we mean by development?
- Who will, in fact, benefit or suffer from a given developmental measure?
- Which are the human ecological principles to be implemented?
- What kind of international collaboration – scientific as well as political – is necessary to reduce the destruction of social and natural systems?

Many open questions remain as to where development and ecology, ethics and policy, concepts and implementation do and should converge. Some of these questions are taken up in the final chapters of this volume under the heading "Consequences for future thinking and action".

PART FOUR
Consequences for future thinking and action

CHAPTER 7
Agrarian culture between conceptual reconstruction and empirics

There has been a continuing debate on rural futures that was nourished in the industrialized world by the agricultural policies of the European Economic Community (EEC) – now European Union (EU) – on the one hand, and on the other by the transfer and application of Green Revolution technologies in the developing world. Two key issues are being discussed: in the field of economics, methods of agricultural production, and at the sociocultural level, the rural way of life. Both have undergone tremendous change, including some unfavourable side-effects, as pointed out on different occasions in the previous chapters.

A novel, alternative concept is that of "rural culture" (*Landkultur*, cf. Bodenstedt 1990) or "agrarian culture" (*Agrarkultur*, cf. Glaeser 1986), which contrasts agri-business with agri-culture and builds upon a cultural concept as opposed to the presently dominant economic concept of foodstuff production cum rural way of life. This approach has a historical component in that it relies on examples from the past and relates historical developments to the present situation in industrialized and developing countries; and it has a normative and political connotation, generating critique and drawing consequences for the future.

"Culture" may be described as "the sum total of social norms or patterns of meaningful action that can be communicated" (Bodenstedt 1990: 36). It is this body of shared knowledge that guides the processes by which humans recognize their environments and that provides them with the necessary confidence to function within and with them. Familiar behaviour and habits produce social and cultural group identity. Rural and urban culture are defined by cultural identity, which shapes the interaction between humans and their natural environment (Bodenstedt 1990: 36–8). This perception relates back to human ecology, as defined in Chapter 1. "Agrarian culture" denotes one specific human ecological sphere, that is that centred around rural food production.

Is rural and/or agrarian culture "a way of life which became obsolete in the wake of industrialization", when the mode of production began to follow industrial norms (Bodenstedt 1990: 46)? The modernization process in agriculture, above all its integration into world market structures by reducing it to a highly specialized and efficient economic subsystem of industrial culture, is observed critically. However, different types of agriculture at local levels are still to be found within the modernized industrial system; Pongratz (1990) analyzes this integration process.

Farmers are often caught in the conflict between tradition and modernity. The combination of traditional and modern demands at which the farming community arrives may provoke the critical question whether modernization is really a one-way, one-dimensional process towards a global monoculture in favour of a dozen high-yielding strains. The necessity to preserve vanishing crop varieties for the sake of human survival has already been recognized. Will this still be possible in a sustainable way when the cultural diversity in which they are grown is extinct? Agricultural and genetic research would gain from a shift from overcoming natural processes to using them – an example for the new intelligent type of modernization that requires less external input and is thus more efficient.

Integrating cultural and agricultural diversity is the main feature of the agrarian culture concept. Agrarian cultures are defined as all forms of sustainable agriculture within existing social and natural environmental constraints, or those forms that have resulted as a reaction to environmental impairment and the tendency towards anomie (absence of social norms or values) in rural societies. Agrarian cultures are regionally limited, accommodated to the natural environment and rooted in the cultural traditions of work, life and the social structures that evolved as forms of "rural society". The subjects of agrarian culture are farmers and peasants; its organization has developed from the traditions of family farming.

According to this definition, agrarian cultures have a double root. The reconstruction of the culture dimension refers to the social and historical origins of culture (as represented in the etymological origin of "colere", to cultivate and to preserve; cf. §7.1); the critical dimension and intention of the concept refers to environmentally and socially destructive impacts (pollution, anomie) of modern economy in general and agriculture in particular; cf. §7.2). Similar approaches in other scientific disciplines include the concept of "moral economy" in cultural anthropology and agricultural economics (Wolff), the concept of "culture core" (Steward), the classical tradition of the Chicago School of human ecology (around Robert Park) and its modern successors (Duncan and others), and the theory of peasant economy (Chayanov). The basic disciplines from which ideas and knowledge flow into the paradigm of agrarian culture are cultural anthropology and theoretical sociology (including the subdisciplines of environmental and rural sociology) and agricultural economics. Strategies for change are discussed in §7.3; §7.4 draws conclusions concerning the consequences for agricultural research.

7.1 Culture and agrarian culture: interrelation or changing relations?

"In the most comprehensive sense, culture is the entirety of manifestations of life, accomplishments and works of a people or groups of peoples" (Schischkoff 1957: 333). The concept comes from the Latin *cultura* meaning "agriculture". In the widest sense, this concept originally meant care, preparation, improvement and perfection of an object for a certain purpose. In the more narrow sense, it meant man's exploitation of nature. Accordingly, the verb *colere* can be interpreted in several ways: to care, to cultivate, to build upon, to form, and to worship through action. Initially it was used to indicate the goal of social cultivation: *agricultura* meant to make the soil useful for human needs.

Analogously, culture also indicated cultivation, and the forming and perfection of human talents and abilities. To this end, Cicero introduced the concept *cultura animi*, the forming of soul and spirit. This concept is identical to that of the Greek *philosophia*, or love of wisdom. *Cultura animi* was later expanded to indicate spiritual development through philosophy, science, ethics and art. In the seventeeth and eighteenth centuries, the bourgeois humanist cultural concept came into being; this brought together all that which humans add to the natural condition in order to arrive at self-perfection. This can be found, for example, in Pufendorf, Adelung and Herder. According to Kant, "Producing in a rational being an aptitude for purposes generally (hence [in a way that leaves] that being free) is *culture*" (Kant 1799, para. 83: 391; 1987: 319).[1] For Kant, then, culture is the ultimate goal of nature with respect to human beings. It realizes itself in morality, in (constituted) bourgeois society, and finally in a "cosmopolitan . . . system of all states", which only wars are in a position to prevent (Kant 1799, para. 83: 393; 1987: 320).

The ever more apparent dissociation of the culture concept from active cultivation to the intellect is reinterpreted in Marxist theory with use of the concept of labour, which frees humans from animalistic dependence on nature. Here, the culture concept encompasses "material and intellectual values produced by humans as prerequisite and basis for further social development . . ." (Klaus & Buhr 1976: 684).

It must be emphasized that in the course of its development the culture concept became ever further removed from its agrarian origins. *Cultura* separated itself, from the eighteenth century onwards, from *agricultura*. This is expressed in the parallel changes that also occurred with the concept agriculture. The agricultural component became separated, for its part, from culture and became "land economy" (the German term *Landwirtschaft* means

---

1. "Die Hervorbringung der Tauglichkeit eines vernünftigen Wesens zu beliebigen Zwecken überhaupt (folglich in seiner Freiheit) ist die Kultur."

agriculture). Here, too, the concept became increasingly narrow until, suddenly, the two concepts found themselves facing each other across a gulf of irreconcilable antagonisms: culture as elitist intellectualism divorced from any real structures, and agriculture as calculated productive activity directed towards individual profit maximization.

For a better understanding of the concept, it may therefore prove useful to regard agrarian culture as a regained component of culture. In so doing, an astonishing series of parallels involuntarily come to mind, all of which must be classified and evaluated. The starting point must be the return of the original concept of culture to an agrarian context. Whenever culture is spoken of – origin, essence, and fate of socialized humans – this involves an evaluation of developmental and historical processes. This applies to agrarian culture as well. Cultural historical observation maintains that there is "development towards an end", either upwards or downwards; or it recognizes that there are recurring cycles. The popular downward-orientated model, since Hesiod, is that of cultural decline from a "golden age" to a "brazen age". A thinker's critique and resignation concerning his contemporary environment are contained in this. An element of it must surely also be in the concept of agrarian culture, when one speaks of its degeneration. Care must be taken, however, to avoid falling into unproductive, retrospective conservatism.

The most enduring of the cultural cycle thinkers was Spengler, whose model of regularly recurring rise and fall was derived from the biological–ecological paradigm (Spengler 1959). "Come into being and pass away" ("*werden und vergehen*") are the metaphors of the balance and flow of nature. The agrarian culture concept goes back directly to the ecological thought model by redesigning the agricultural system into an agro-ecosystem, that is into an agrarian system that imitates natural cycles and uses them to its own end.

The idea of constant upward development, based on Christian eschatological concepts, reached a point of culmination in Hegel and Marx. Reflection upon one's own culture in historical sequence and in comparison to others' revealed its relativeness as one among many. "The culture" as an uninterrupted unity was replaced by the plurality of cultures. The agrarian culture concept is in the process of replicating this leap. Whereas it seemed, thus far, that there has been only one industrialized, globally orientated agriculture in contrast to primitive, regional methods of cultivation, we may now speak of agricultures in the plural, as specifically agrarian arrangements proper to diverse cultures.

In view of the interrelations sketched above, the definition of "culture" as an object of scientific observation seems somewhat strained. A concept characterized by constant change is very difficult to delimit. The deeper cognitive reason for this is the unsuccessful attempt to nail down an historical process through static concept formulation, that is ahistorically. One alternative method for getting a better grip on the meaning of culture and its mutability would be to contrast it with its respective opposites. The basic meaning of the culture concept is hidden in the dominant language usage of agricultural science, for instance, in the concepts "strawberry cultivation" "tree and shrub cultivation", or "cultivated land". Culture refers here to the opposite concept, "nature": natural conditions that have been altered through tilling or livestock breeding.

Further, other concepts came into being such as "cultural landscape", "people of a certain culture" (in German *Kulturvolk*, meaning "civilized nation") or "cultured person", as opposed to unspoiled nature, primitive people (*Naturvolk*), or "child of nature". Culture is regarded as the "natural environment" of humans, in contrast to nature as the natural environment of animals. Culture in opposition to nature is thus brought closer to intellect; "cultural sciences" (Rickert) are identical to *Geisteswissenschaften* (humanities).[2]

Cultural critique starts with this dichotomy, whether in the form of Rousseau's turning to the natural ideal, or Marxist cultural materialism, which strives to reduce culture to its material, that is economic basis, and draw from it: culture as the superstructure of (class) social relations. For what, then, does agrarian cultural critique strive? As with every cultural critique, it is "a process of social self-orientation and new consciousness vis-à-vis the cultural whole, mainly in rejecting the present and factual, and in placing emphasis on and raising older cultural forms of Utopian cultural ideals to the level of absolute cultural norms" (Diemer & Frenzel 1958: 127).

The dangers of the restorative tendency and a romanticizing conservatism appear to be genuine. They can be eliminated through the method of critical historical analysis of the problems that will emerge from the world economic system in the foreseeable future and the accompanying divergences and conflicts of interest. A political evaluation on the basis of clearly laid out goal intentions is desirable and also necessary on the part of those scientists whose responsibility it is to contribute to the development of social emancipation.

7.2 Agrarian culture with political intentions: some case examples

Agrarian cultural critique is occasioned by discontent with current agrarian policy (Priebe 1985), beginning with the European Community/Union right through the Green Revolution; a policy that – along with the undeniable increases in productivity in some areas – has brought with it economic

---

2. For further elaboration on some of the concepts of nature in relation to culture, see Chapter 8.

discrepancies, social dissolution, ecological impoverishment, and a lowering of the cultural level (Pufendorf 1986). The catch-words and negative characteristics in the industrialized countries are growth fetishism and over-production, the squandering of financial and natural resources, including energy, subventionism and protectionism with related negative effects on developing countries, such as displacement competition at the subsistence level alongside declining sales at the monetary level. These interrelations point to "industrialization" and "colonialism" as the real causes for the conceptual changes in culture and agriculture mentioned above – depending in each case on whether the development under consideration is in the industrialized world or the world on its periphery.

Pig-fattening in many areas in the European Union, for example, has become dependent on tapioca, which is produced from cassava that, in turn, is imported from the developing countries. What does this mean for the "agrarian culture" of local farmers, this dependency on plants that are not a product of one's own tilling of the soil? What effects does this development of an agrarian culture of industrialized growth societies have on the emergence of contradictions in rural inhabitants' structures of consciousness, on farmers' attitudes towards their own history, work or power relations?

A farm household's sense of self-esteem is often in strange contrast to its inhabitants' lack of historical consciousness. The history of one's own family or one's own farmhouse is often unknown. Belief in progress and technology dominates; farmer conservatism seems to be a thing of the past. The farmer has switched roles and become a manager of the land (*Landwirt*) (Buntzel 1986). Local historical awareness can still only be found in sentimental customary rituals and in traditional national or home-town organizations.

European Union agrarian policy forms the background of these changes in behaviour. Today, the only chance of survival on many smaller full-time farms is in increasing pig output with the help of imported feed. An immense hunger for land, caused by uncertainty as to prospects for the future, and the menace imposed by the "grow or go" alternative is the result. The pressure towards increasing land use is facilitated by machine plants, oversized as they are.

This hunger for land extends into the developing countries as well. Cassava has conquered a significant segment of the world market in animal feed. Thailand, especially, has become one of the most important exporters of animal feed to the European Union. Here, one can see the change from agrarian cultural to worldwide economic use and the resulting conflict. For the inhabitants and the land in which cassava monoculture extends over large areas and long periods of time, this can mean destabilization of basic foodstuff production, enormous ecological damage, and increasing dependency and impoverishment of small farmers (Franke 1986). Before unification the Federal Republic of Germany imported about 80 per cent of its concentrates from the Third World, only to produce mountains of butter and lakes of milk, while using large purchasing power to force out producers of human food in the Third World. This negative development worsens with increasing intensive farming and mass animal husbandry. The natural cycle is disrupted, nutrition and waste management occur according to anti-ecological principles of industrialized production. Excessive use of medicines and artificial fatteners also poses a threat to human health.

Another example of the displacement effects of competition on basic food production is sugar. Worldwide increases in sugar production have resulted in the oversupply of a product that is largely superfluous and often damaging (Leitzmann et al. 1986); on the other hand, traditional agriculture, which produces foodstuffs essential to healthy human development, is forced out of business. In Brazil, for example, sugar-cane production to meet energy and export needs forces out the cultivation of basic foodstuffs. The results are soil degradation, dangers brought about by the increased use of pesticides, and disruption of social structures from sugar producers' modern agricultural strategies. This also creates problems related to nutritive physiology for the consumer in the form of tooth decay, diabetes, sugar-related malnourishment and obesity.

On the whole, increased purchasing power in the industrialized countries has resulted in a trend towards consumption patterns based on processed and "refined" foods. This applies to refined sugar and white flour as well as to vegetables, fruit, cheese, eggs and meat, whereas the consumption of (unprocessed) potatoes, grain products, peas and beans has declined sharply. According to the German Federal Government's 1980 report on nutrition, excessive energy intake is the reason why 30–50 per cent of the country's citizens are overweight, whereas, on the other hand, a 500 million people in the countries of the Third World suffer from hunger. Differences in purchasing power are the cause of differences in distribution, and not insufficient supplies or production bottlenecks. In the industrial countries, a quarter of grain production is used for animal feed; only 10 per cent is consumed directly. Processing losses due to the transformation of plant into animal calories are 80–90 per cent.

Early changes in agrarian cultures were caused not only by industrialization, but also by colonialism. Whatever was needed in the motherland was produced in the colonies, irrespective of local needs and socio-economic patterns. One example of this is the decline of the Sahel culture, which was caused by various forms of colonialism. In 5000 BC plants had been domesticated in the Sahel zone of West Africa; it was home to 25 cultivated plants that are still in use today. Arabic sources indicate the earlier existence of great empires in this area (Gana, Mali and Gao) before and after Arabian colonization in the seventh century. Chroniclers describe flowering agrarian cultures with a diversity of cultivating techniques in harmony with animal husbandry and trade. During the course of Arabian colonialism, the grains that were adapted to the arid climate became less popular. The upper strata of society ate imported wheat and rice. Thus, not only was the land conquered; living and farming habits changed as well. The society declined, the soil degraded, and hunger spread with the onset of the slave trade in the early sixteenth century (Imfeld 1986a). Nineteenth century colonialism introduced monocultures; with the rise of national states beginning in 1960, the successive external colonialization was replaced by an internal one.

Another example of this kind of change can been seen in the crisis of pastoralism (Imfeld 1986a): the overgrazing of fields. Prestige considerations, modern veterinary medicine, or the lack of meat markets are held to be responsible for this. The main cause, however, appears to lie in external colonial influences. Men were pressed into service; children forced to go to school. The lack of shepherds left no alternative other than to concentrate herds. Knowledge of herd management techniques, including dividing herds at the right time, has declined.

Finally, there is the case of maize, an apparently typically African cultivated plant that is the product of the slave and colonial days. This food, which is easily transported and stored, enabled long-distant transportation of humans in the first place. Africans were forced to plant maize, which then supplanted millet and sorghum. Maize has become established in the meantime, and the task is now to "decolonialize" it. This means that monoculture has to be reduced and more emphasis placed on diversity, change and new networking (Imfeld 1986b). An adaptation to the demands of nutrition physiology has thus far occurred as seldom as the adaptation to African soils or climates.

With the onset of the forced opening of the country to rising Japanese imperialism – to take an example from Asia – Korea's agrarian culture began to decline. Korea's transformation into Japan's first foreign market ruined the domestic rural-based cottage industry. After the formal colonialization in 1910, the expansion of large landownership was accompanied by the annulment of farmers' rights of tenancy. In addition, agriculture was monetarized. Taxes had to be paid in currency. Seeds and commercial fertilizers had to be imported from Japan. The traditional form of exploitation, tribute, was replaced by the market economy, in order to promote capital accumulation. It was to this same end that food prices were kept low by cheap imports. This resulted in the establishment of a dual economic structure: the internal market supported the export sector. It should be kept in mind, however, that the decisive attack on Korean agrarian culture occurred (in the south of Korea) only after the liberation from Japan. Land reform was carried out during the American occupation, and this transferred, for all time, the form of exploitation of the farmers from tribute to the market price mechanism. Cheap supplies of labour and raw materials served an "export dictatorship". The farmers' need for money resulted in even mutual help being monetarized (Kim & Michel-Kim 1986). In the meantime, young people began to see their futures in the city. Despair has paralysed village life.

These examples show that the conceptual reconstruction of agrarian culture, developed with the help of empirical accounts as well as those derived from an analysis of secondary sources, is located within the context of political economic change. Thus the two roots of agrarian culture become clear. The concept of agrarian culture, or cultures, presented here was gained from the conceptual historical reconstruction and synthesis of the origins of the culture concept. Its legitimacy, on the other hand, is derived from its generation of critique and from the actual consequences the change has brought about for the world economic system, deemed to be unsatisfactory in that they are harmful to humans and the environment. Agrarian culture, which is an heuristic concept, strives to make visible an originally greater wealth of relations, not in order to return to the origins, but in order to work out that which has been lost and, in so doing, make it useful for future development. The expansion of theoretical dimensions has its consequences for the diversity of agropolitical options, and thus merges with the strategies of holistic human ecology as opposed to those of sectoral agricultural policy limited to mere reductionist behaviour.

7.3 Strategies for change

It would appear that to expound on the concept of agrarian culture is a far easier exercise than to try to locate its characteristic norms, values, and their respective behaviour patterns in the past and transfer them in a use-orientated way to the future. This seems to be the essential characteristic of agrarian culture in Europe (Bodenstedt 1986). It is indeed much easier to formulate a critique of the course taken by modern agricultural development and to demand that this course be reversed, than it is to prove historically which past agricultural goals and values should be pursued in the future. The reason for this difficulty lies in the critical question of evaluation, that is whether our ancestors' culture and agrarian culture can be deemed to have been better or worse than those of today. Change and resistance to change have always been two equally possible social developments. If change resulting from more powerful foreign influences gains the upper hand, the threat of loss of cultural identity arises. If resistance dominates, stagnation threatens. What remains is often the question of which standard is used.

In order to return to the question of economic and cultural polarity, therefore: should we desire the conservative farmer, or the farmer-entrepreneur who believes in progress? In fact, both worlds of consciousness are valid today. This contradiction has driven entire rural populations to a near schizophrenic state. Modernity and urban models have won out in consumer behaviour as well as in municipal policy. On the other hand, traditional patterns of behaviour and value systems dominate in the areas of matrimony,

134

family, education, sexuality and politics. It must be kept in mind, however, that the "split consciousness of the farmers . . . also corresponds to the objective schizophrenic nature of their economic condition" (Buntzel 1986: 40), which is divided between industrial rationalization and loving and self-sacrificing activity. For this reason, there is indeed no united resistance against rural power relations: "The farmer faces giant companies both as a tiny demand factor on the farm machinery market and a tiny supply factor on the agricultural products market . . ." (Buntzel 1986: 42). The agricultural press and rural adult education provide no enlightenment here. Exploitative relations are maintained for as long as the farmer remains imprisoned in traditional structures of thought. For the same reason, but with a guilty conscience, violations are committed against nature; this explains the especially sharp reaction to ecological criticism: such criticism hits home.

Is the ecological question perhaps the key, or at least an important indicator, of agricultural degradation and, thus, also an instrument for forming new attitudes and change? In view of the overwhelmingly large numbers of sources of harm and dangers in the industrialized countries, there are many indications that this could indeed be the case. The developing countries have already been affected to such an extent, however, that the very health and life of entire groups of people is threatened as a result of the importation and use of pesticides that have long since been prohibited in the countries where they are produced.

As the starting point for an alternative agricultural and development concept, then, ecology can only be understood politically in the sense of a "political ecology". Development itself is a political concept that – in the industrialized as well as in the developing countries – depends on economic pressure and the sociocultural context of interrelations that, for their part, also exist in the interaction of domestic and foreign policy decisions.

In the agrarian area, ecologically suited methods of production, in short ecofarming, form the agrotechnical application of ecodevelopment. With the help of locally adapted, circulation-orientated production, ecofarming maintains and increases soil fertility, which is based on soil quality, water supply and bio-ecological potential. Use is made especially of an ecosystem's natural forces, whereas conventional agriculture is dependent on an incomparably greater use of energy and capital, and in addition contaminates the environment through the use of agrochemicals (Rottach 1988).

7.4 Conclusion

"Agrarian culture" or "agri-culture" refers to alternative methods of agriculture to profit-orientated, market-based, environmentally destructive forms of intensive agriculture in the sense of "agri-business". Agrarian culture focuses on the social and cultural subjects of farming (e.g. the family farming tradition and peasantry as the social subject of agriculture) in contrast to agriculture in its modern form, which has developed more and more into agribusiness, that is, profit- and market-orientated agricultural production with an economic subject: the market.

In the scientific discourse, four variations of the concept of agrarian culture can be found. Emphasis is placed on the latter two of those listed below (Bruckmeier and Teherani-Krönner 1992: 3–4):

- *Historical denotation:* Agrarian culture was related to the historical forms and traditions of agriculture before the technical and economic modernization processes under modern capitalism.
- *Romantic connotation:* The implicit or explicit normative connotation of agrarian culture is that of a way of life in harmony with nature, of non-alienated, creative work.
- *Ethical denotation:* Agrarian culture is agriculture according to normative or cultural standards rooted in the ethics of being part of nature. The ethics of agrarian culture are of responsibility for man and environment, sustainable use of natural resources, subsistence production before market production, orientation towards value in use instead of commodity production (cf. Ch. 3).
- *Ecological connotation:* This refers to a practical orientation of agrarian culture towards environmentally sound agriculture, that is agriculture in practice as protection of the environment, landscape and nature.

Ecological connotation, resulting from a critique of the disastrous economic and ecological consequences of modern agriculture in First and Third World countries, is the actual point of departure.

Versions of the agrarian culture concept are often linked as follows:

- A combination of historical denotation with romantic connotation. The result is a retrospective ideology targeting a prospective Utopia with a traditional bias and favouring cultural values.
- A combination of ethical denotation with ecological connotation. This is represented by a concept of sustainable development (or ecodevelopment) in agriculture with an ethical valuation of agriculture as the inviolable art of human survival.

It has become apparent that not even the generally accepted conceptualizations can be applied critically any longer, since they contain untested ideological elements. Thus the term "world nourishment" assumes in undertones and as a self-evident fact agrarian policies of the Green Revolution and the European Union that are no longer acceptable: a world market strategy for reducing surpluses while destroying mature, regionally specific social, economic and ecological structures; dissolution of diversity through "monocultures" in the ecological as well as the socio-economic sphere.

In dealing with the causes of the Gordian knot of the agro-industrial complex's economic interests, of immovable national and transnational administrations, and of science as ideology; complex historical interrelations become apparent, such as industrialization and the rise of capitalist behaviour patterns, colonialism and economies of slavery, cultural imperialism and unreflected technology transfer.

In other words, alternative suggestions concerning food policy can only scratch the surface of a deep-seated tumour, unless it can make the structural interrelations visible. Out of this emerge at least the beginnings of a threefold parallel and interwoven task for future research:

- pointing out structures typical of agrarian maldevelopment,
- research into historical causes, and
- critical evaluation of all concepts usually employed in order to detect ideological components.

The last point forms the conceptual cornerstone: agrarian culture replaces agriculture, which is a concept that has become ideologically and politically strained. Agrarian culture thus becomes the symbol for regaining complex cultural interrelations and, hence, economic, ecological and social diversity. A novel way of observing and thinking poses the challenge of a reorientating agrarian, as well as agropolitical, behaviour (Groeneveld 1986). The danger of being overcome by misunderstandings concerning neo-conservatism, hostility towards economics or science, has been recognized and will hopefully be avoided. On the contrary, in order to prevent further, perhaps deadly, damage from occurring to the biosphere, it is necessary to incorporate technology with humans and nature and, in so doing, arrive at a metamorphosis of the societies of industrial growth.

The general hypothesis is that the reduction of pollution and ecological change in agriculture is not only a technical problem with regard to production techniques; to some important degree, it is a problem of culture and cultural change that cannot be managed or influenced directly or instrumentally, for example through regulatory, political action. At more detailed levels, three questions should be answered:

- How can agricultural production systems become more integrated ecologically at the farm and regional level to avoid environmental impairment from production processes (not just by the use of end-of-pipe technologies)?
- Which cultural orientations, ways of life and forms of production among the agricultural population support or imply environmentally sound use of natural resources?
- Which groups of farmers and social agents can take the role of avant-gardes or become subjects in the processes of developing new agrarian cultures?

These questions can only be answered within a framework of theoretical and empirical sociological analysis. The cultural and social aspects of agricultural environmental problems – for example the social perception of such problems, the forms of land- and water use, the normative and symbolic valuation of landscape and nature – are self-evident. Nevertheless, this has not been taken into consideration adequately in environmental discussion of agriculture in political or scientific contexts. There, emphasis should be placed on the sociocultural conditions of agriculture. The factors influencing environmentally related action have to be reconstructed within a holistic approach to agriculture as a sociocultural system.

CHAPTER 8

Nature in crisis?
A cultural misunderstanding

Is the so-called environmental crisis actually a cultural crisis? If so, what exactly does "environmental crisis" mean in this case? If the use of the term is justified, what factors might have led to the conditions to which it refers? Are these ideological factors – in the sense of the history of ideas – rather than interest-bound matters? Is the "environmental crisis", therefore, an "ideological crisis" and, in this sense, a crisis of our culture? What is the essence of the link between environment and nature, the interdependence between nature and culture, upon which our sense of "crisis" is based? The following reflections attempt to answer these questions.

Enlightenment and emancipation, identified as natural science and social science Utopias, were the impetus behind the successful development of modern Europe. Following disillusionment with Utopian ideals, the negative side of "successful development" has become apparent: success was gained at the expense of nature and the environment; humankind is under threat (§8.1). In the face of endangerment, the dual nature of the species *Homo sapiens* between nature and culture becomes manifest. After bringing into question some of the tenets of natural philosophy and, at the same time, observing practice in everyday life, one can conclude that "nature", as a thing in itself, does not exist for human beings. Humans have specific concepts of nature, which correspond to different behavioural precepts; these, in turn, can be formalized as ethical codes. Such concepts of nature can be described as culturally determined; they result from our limited human cognitive faculty that functions as a filter. The paradoxical conclusion that can be drawn from these deliberations is, that, whereas culture is a product of natural evolution, nature is a construct of culture (§8.2).

What follows, then, is an attempt to resolve this contradiction. First, the "unity of nature and culture" is investigated from the perspective of "universal history", based upon theconcept of evolution; secondly, it is re-examined from the perspective of "cultural ecology", based upon the concept of culture. Finally, human ecology is considered as a related approach to the universal history and cultural ecology approaches; its similarities to and divergences from these approaches are scrutinized (§8.3).

The penultimate section of this chapter (§8.4) concludes, on the basis of foregoing deliberations, that there is no "crisis in nature". It contends that talk of "crisis in nature" is, contrary to what we may believe, far more an indication of a cultural crisis in our society. Nevertheless, humankind's intuitive, that is anthropocentric interest in its own survival, demands that societal behaviour with regard to nature be changed, that *Homo sapiens* treat nature with care. The conclusion here – ironically – is that correct behaviour towards nature is not always based on correct thinking about nature.

8.1 Technological development, social emancipation and their limitations

Modern Utopias

Modern history has given rise to two great Utopian ideals that differ fundamentally both in their emancipatory power and in their hubris from all earlier dreams of humankind. The first of these Utopian ideals – let us call it the *natural science* Utopia – claims that humankind, through the use of science and technology, will be able to liberate itself from nature, its arch-enemy and oppressor since banishment from Paradise. Descartes was one of the main representatives of the scientific Utopian approach. With unprecedented rigour, he developed a two-class model of the universe, consisting of extended, physical objects (*res extensa*) and cognition (*res cogitans*). As one of the founders of mathematical science, he laid the foundations for a major upheaval in the traditional relations between humans and nature: Cartesian dualism helped place the thinking being hierarchically above the extended reality, that is man over nature.

The second Utopian ideal – I shall call it the *social science* Utopia – postulates that human society consists of two major contingents: those who sell their labour and those who own the means of production. The former can liberate themselves from the latter, their oppressors since the age of industrialization, by self-determination of their own labour, that is controlling the means of production. The social science Utopian ideal is associated above all with Karl Marx, who introduced a two-class model of society based upon the ownership or non-ownership of the means of production. Marx developed a value theory of labour that, together with his concept of "class struggle", laid the foundations for overcoming traditional power relations in society.

Both the natural science and the social science Utopias were characterized by enlightenment. The common goal was emancipation and liberation. Proponents of these philosophies unmasked their opponents as oppressors by means of the critique of ideology. This was done, on the one hand, by arguing against traditional religious beliefs, declaring the priests to be deceivers in favour of the mighty; and, on the other hand, by arguing that it was the social being (*Sein*), that is one's adherence to either the upper or the lower social class, that determined consciousness (*Bewußtsein*).

Both Utopian ideals were the driving forces behind social development far into the twentieth century, not only in Europe and in those countries at the end of the first stage of technological and economic industrialization, but throughout the world. The motivation has been the desire for a better life – the greatest happiness for the greatest number – or the need to catch up economically with the North. But these Utopian ideals have since been called into question. Doubts are being expressed about their ability to enlighten and emancipate. What is the cause of this criticism?

As the twentieth century comes to a close, we are facing a general threat to life. Uncontrolled armament, including the increased production of nuclear weapons throughout most of the century, have been a major contributor to present problems. Pressure on the environment has meant the destruction of the last natural preserves, which had, up to now, been spared. The industrial countries, particularly in the East, are facing economic stagnation, unemployment and increasing social instability, and a widespread feeling that there is "no future". The developing nations have become economically dependent on the industrialized nations in their attempts to modernize and enter into the world market. Their indebtedness has spiralled upwards at a phenomenal rate, impoverishing these nations structurally. Human beings are becoming marginalized in society as a result of large-scale technological development; the preponderance of information and communication technologies threatens to streamline society into a general, nondescript uniformity. Time is no longer a pleasantly flowing stream bringing us innovations that promise happiness, but "a limited resource for the future-orientated mastering of problems" (Habermas 1985: 141).

The end of the history of nature? Three theses

How have things come to be this way? Three hypotheses follow, in which I attempt to explain these developments.

THESIS 1: THE EFFECTS OF TECHNOLOGICAL DEVELOPMENT ARE CONTRADICTORY

As an instrument of power, technology conflicts with the original goals of emancipation. The more complex a system becomes, the more unclear it becomes how to control the system. Competent control of the system in question diminishes and dysfunctional consequences begin to take over. Weapons technology, for instance, has given rise to a destructive power of previously unknown proportions, threatening the survival of the biosphere. Progress in genetic and biological engineering will soon be able to make it possible not only to alter human nutritional conditions, but also humankind itself. Communication and information technology can already be used by states to establish complete control over their citizens. The tendency as well is towards complete control over natural and societal development. Although the forces of nature have been successfully harnessed, liberating humankind to an incredible extent, emancipation has not been achieved: societal controls have transformed it into its opposite. The scientific Utopia as enlightenment has failed to a great extent.

THESIS 2: THE LIBERATION OF LABOUR FROM EXTERNAL DOMINANCE HAS NOT SUCCEEDED

The labour-based industrial society is stagnating. Technology created the conditions for mass production and mass affluence, and, at the same time laid the foundation for heteronomous labour and the "disfranchisement" of nature. Characteristic of industrialized production is high productivity at the expense of the autonomy of labour, and the exploitation of nature. The goal of the social science Utopian ideal was self-determination (*Selbstbestimmung*) in one's work, which later, under reformist union policies, became self-determination outside one's work in terms of growing leisure-time activities. Marx's original model failed because the expropriation of the expropriators did not in any way lead automatically to the liberation of the working classes from external domination (*Fremdbestimmung*). The reformist model is also being judged with increasing scepticism, because in the heteronomous area of labour (self-determination outside of, rather than within one's sphere of work) neither full employment nor social welfare for all can be guaranteed ("the illusion of the welfare state": Koslowski 1985: 801); and in the area of leisure, autonomy is often little more than a vacuous promise, becoming in turn a new source for the exploitation of nature (mass tourism, the leisure-time industry). Thus, little remains of the enlightenment–emancipatory impetus of social science Utopian ideals.

THESIS 3: THE MORE EFFECTIVELY WE LEARN TO CONTROL NATURE, THE MORE NATURE – IN ITS IMPOTENCY – STRIKES BACK AT US

A new problem has arisen that, since the end of the 1960s, can no longer be ignored. In the labour-based industrial society, mass production relying on modern science and technology is leading to the destruction of nature. What began with local and regional ecosystems has now reached global proportions. We have retained some aspect of Cartesian dualism in that we tend to divide all of nature into two parts: humankind, the thinking part, and the environment, the extended part. The endangering of the environment, for which the term "pollution" is far too innocuous, means a real threat to humankind, because it attacks the basis for health and survival. This threat to "peace with nature" (Meyer-Abich 1984a) implies a threat to all humankind, be it by warfare, economic exploitation, or poisoning the environment. The end of nature's history means the end of human history. Therefore, the final outcrop of our natural science and social science Utopian ideals in the modern age is fear for our own (continued) existence.

8.2 The dual nature of *Homo sapiens*

The natural paradox of man

Nature, in Latin *natura*, comes from *nasci*: to be born, to emerge. The corresponding Greek terms *physis* and *phyein* are similarly related to each other. Nature is, therefore, "everything that emerges without external influence and which develops according to its own immanent powers and laws" (Hoffmeister 1955: 421 f.). It is its linguistic origin that has led occasionally to the confusing ambiguity of the concept of nature. On the one hand, "nature" refers to the character of an object, that is to that which is essential to the existence of the object, its "core" (inner nature, essence). On the other hand, "nature" refers to the whole of reality, that is that which has come about independent of human action and which is subject only to natural laws (external nature, the world, universe).

In the context of the environmental crisis it is above all external, "physical" nature (this is actually a pleonasm) that interests us. Here, too, complications arise from the origin of the concept. External nature is contrasted with "what human beings have created", that is with everything that specifically pertains to human beings – for instance, mind, culture, civilization, history – as opposed to other organisms. The difficulty results from the fact that human beings as a species are themselves part of external nature and that every individual possesses, not of his/her own making, a blueprint for development and the requisite potential of growth.

> As long as I am identical with nature I understand what living nature is just as I understand my own life; . . . but as soon as . . . I separate myself from nature nothing remains for me but a dead object, and I cease to understand how life outside myself is possible. (Schelling 1967 [1797]: 47 f.)

Therefore, the idea of an absolute separation of culture and nature is not cogent: it presupposes that culture is non-natural, since it (culture) is a human creation; but, human beings are themselves a part of nature.

Previously in the history of philosophy use was made of a variety of dichotomies involving all existing things, which, it was claimed, belonged either to the class of "extended" objects or the class of "thinking" objects

(Descartes); and it was argued, moreover, that human beings – similarly divided up – were dualistic in nature: consisting of matter *and* mind, or body *and* spirit. Today, however, such conceptual crutches seem obsolete to us, if only because our ontology has become more complex. Dualistic models that purport to categorize everything that exists in terms of "extension" and "thought" seem hopelessly naïve today.

> Since quantum theory takes the idea seriously that matter as extended substance is defined by cognizability, and consciousness as the thinking substance is defined by cognition, the inevitable question arises as to what these two supposedly different substances have to do with each other. (Weizsäcker 1989: 22 f.)

In addition, God as Creator has come to play an increasingly diminished role: *natura naturans*, active, creative nature, is left to organize itself. The reconstruction of this process is called "evolution", the history of nature. The natural paradox of humankind comes into even sharper focus here: humankind emerged as a result of the evolutionary process, but its *differentia specifica* as the species *Homo sapiens* – mind, history, culture –are supposedly completely dissociated from this process, indeed, they are said to represent the embodiment of its antithesis. The question is, then, does culture stand in irresolvable opposition to nature?

Nature as a cultural concept

Let us first consult natural philosophy (Diemer & Frenzel 1967: 186–209; Stöckler 1989: 1–18). The aim of natural philosophers is to interpret and explain nature. Their subject is the unification of our knowledge of nature, and the clarification of fundamental scientific concepts and the laws of natural processes. They attempt to answer the question: "What is reality?" (Drieschner 1981: 4/14). The term "natural philosophy" in the Anglo-Saxon tradition means the theoretical, mathematical foundation of the empirical, quantitative natural sciences. Natural philosophers are thus primarily dependent upon the specific level of scientific development that historically had emerged out of natural philosophy.

Fundamental to contemporary natural science, in addition to the theory of relativity and quantum mechanics – physical theories whose development has decisively influenced our view of nature – is the theory of evolution. From the perspective of biology there is no reason to exclude "mind" from evolution; on the contrary, the "evolution of mind" is held to be a special achievement of evolution (Drieschner 1981: 125 f.). Culture, therefore, is a definite part of the natural process, at least in terms of its emergence.

From the perspective of biology, humankind is embedded in nature in a threefold manner, as its product, its user, and as its master (Markl 1986: 7). It follows then that humankind has a duty to care for and preserve nature, that is that nature's preservation is a "cultural obligation" (Markl 1986: 9).

> For more than three billion years the Earth has housed life. One of its inhabitants – the species *Homo sapiens* – together with its biological slaves has taken over the dwelling. . . . But this success is . . . not without cost: it obliges us to assume active responsibility for keeping the Earth inhabitable. (Markl 1986: 354)

Based upon experience in Western industrial society, we can say that the permanent environmental crisis has led to individual as well as group demands that we respect nature and that "creation be preserved" – in short, that man has obligations with regard to nature. Let us call such concepts "ethicized concepts of nature". An ethicized concept of nature ascribes moral status to nature and, in so doing, insists upon correction of commonly accepted patterns of modernization. It requires that we abandon anthropocentric moral concepts and that we turn away from a natural science-centred culture (van den Daele 1992: 41).

This is, of course, not the dominant concept of nature in industrial societies. The by far more widely held view, based upon many interests, sees nature first and foremost as a source of raw materials. This concept sanctions and encourages the economic exploitation of nature within the framework of continued expansion of technological capability; it creates and promotes the social illusion of unlimited growth and unlimited material wellbeing. This view appeals to modern science for its justification.

Concepts of nature based on successful industrial development and ethicized concepts of nature generated in reaction to the injurious consequences of nature *qua* resource for unlimited exploitation are really just two sides of the same coin. Their common ground is the successful imposition of the mathematical sciences on natural phenomena. With the domination of number, time and space over nature, nature and technology have become congruent.

To proclaim the preservation of nature as a cultural obligation is an ethical postulate. It presupposes a particular concept of nature and a corresponding ethical demand as to how one ought to behave towards nature. But, we are not compelled to accept that particular concept of nature nor are we compelled to accept the ethical postulate. This suggests that other concepts of nature and behaviour with regard to it are conceivable.

Completely different concepts of nature, resulting in different orientations towards nature, emerge with the use of other "languages". Examples of such alternative nature semantics can be found in the aesthetic intuitive perception of nature, as well as in mystical or religious communion with nature. Another example of an alternative concept of nature is the idea of nature as a threat – a still commonplace view. Such things as perils associated with the open sea, earthquakes, volcanoes, areas protected by dikes – to mention only a few – all attest to the terror that nature can spread.

That the paradigm of humankind's domination over nature is limited is well illustrated by farmers in temperate regions whose crops still depend upon the weather, despite all the resources of science. These farmers must still decide whether, for instance, they will harvest their grain today when it is sunny, or let it continue to ripen – at the risk of their crop through a sudden burst of rain tomorrow. People on all continents, who live close to nature (such as Alpine shepherds, Amazonian campesinos, Sahelian nomads, small farmers in tropical regions eking out a living on land threatened by erosion) have learned to accept living with the perils of nature, rather than attempting to dominate it, precisely because of their immediate dependence upon its exploitation. From this we can see that different concepts of nature result from culturally determined differences in dealing with nature for the sake of survival: nature is a cultural concept.

The cultural filter and the renewal of the natural paradox

The answer to the question, "What is nature?", must be different from that found in the philosophical tradition, because the question is being asked semantically rephrased. "Nature" by itself does not exist; rather, it is the result of our access to it. Nature is just the process of experiencing nature, that is, it is a construct of culture. This does not mean that nature is not "real": rather, it means that all reality is "experienced" reality that has been previously passed through human feeling, perception and thought (including scientific experimentation). If one imagines the human capacity for experience (including every sort of internal and external perception) to be a net, then reality for human beings is only that which can be trapped in this net (Dürr 1989: 29 f.). Popper expresses this idea as follows:

> Theory is the net that we throw out to catch "the world" – to make it rational, to explain and become master of it. We are endeavouring to make the mesh of the net finer and finer. (Popper 1982 [1934]: 31)

Deeper realities or other realities may exist, but it is not possible to say anything about them. In a literary style, this can be expressed as follows. "Continually surfing on the crests of our unhealthy logical habits and our planetary limitations, of our adaption to a certain temperature scale, within which one can speak of something like 'solid bodies' and things" (Gustafsson 1989: 104) means that we are dependent upon our biologically given cognitive capacity. The net of experience – keeping to the metaphor – is woven out of a myriad of differently coloured, cultural threads. This is what is meant when one says that nature is a cultural construct: it is the culturally imbued concept of nature through which every experience of nature is filtered. To reiterate more poetically,

> No wonder that the world is so surprisingly colourful, variable, mysterious, and meaningful. It is we ourselves who have made it so variegated. What a terrifying monotony the real world has in comparison with ours! It has acquired colour, but we were the colourists! The human mind has made it possible for the world of phenomena to emerge, and has exported them into the grey world of being . . .
> (Gustafsson 1989: 104)

Our analysis up to this point has led to two contradictory results: first, culture is a part of nature; secondly, nature is a construct of culture. The reasoning appears to be circular: that is, that culture as a part of nature makes it possible for us to experience nature by constructing it. But is this a contradiction?

What would seem at first glance to be a contradiction results from the particular perspective from which each statement has emerged. These statements signify particular concepts of culture and nature that draw their meaning from their relationship to each other. More intriguing than the difference between the two statements, however, is what they have in common. This becomes clear when one considers them side by side. The common ground underlying these statements is the assumption that nature and culture are bound together in such a way that each concept is meaningless without the other, although the priorities are different. The unity of nature and culture is the common, general thesis, and it is diametrically opposed to the scientific concept that has dominated since the nineteenth century. Two possible perspectives arise here: the concept of the unity of nature and culture within nature, and the unity of nature and culture within culture. Significant attempts at describing this unity are to be found in the approaches of "universal history" and "cultural ecology".

8.3 Attempts to resolve the contradiction

The unity of nature and culture within nature: the universal history approach

The universal history approach associates nature with culture through the concept of evolution (Sieferle 1989: 44–6). Here the notion of ecosystem as an heuristic concept permits the application of the ideas of systems theory to animate nature. The assumption is made, in accordance with the science of ecology, that the transformation of ecological systems represents the normal history of the Earth. This means that equilibrium enjoys no more privileged a status than disequilibrium. Transformation can be brought about biotically or abiotically. The evolution of organisms is biotic: it is explained in neo-Darwinism by means of the interplay between genetic variation (reproduction errors resulting from transcription mistakes) and environmentally determined selection (the struggle for life).

Human beings bring a new quality to the evolutionary process: "cultural evolution". They learn by trial and error, and can pass on their experience directly to future generations, bypassing genetic transformation. This is the basis for cultural development, the rapidity of which proceeds more and more desynchronously than the evolutionary rate of all other species. As a consequence, the possibility for human intervention into ecosystems has emerged, and this can lead to such rapid and complete change that the result would be wholly destructive.

Culture is, therefore, a concept within organic evolution – a concept of unity with nature within nature. Like nature, culture organizes itself. The breathtaking speed of the cultural process of self-organization is the reason for humankind's extraordinary position in nature. Within the global ecosystem, the biosphere, and its far more slowly paced rate of self-organization, this special position results in both friction and destruction. It is in terms of these two processes that culture, not the biological species *Homo sapiens*, is the subject of the evolutionary process. "One of culture's elementary achievements must be to materially preserve its human carrier" (Sieferle 1989: 47).

One criticism of the methodology of universal history has been that it conceives of natural history and human history as parallel phenomena and, in so doing, obscures the specific differences between them. The concept of history, it is claimed, "loses its contours" and the specific quality of human history, that of there being "room for change", gets lost (Kluge & Schramm 1989: 57 f.). In short, universal history as the unity of nature and culture within nature is rejected as the "naturalizing" of history, because the natural core of history reduces history's cultural aspects to the contingent, the accidental and the marginal. Moreover, critics of the universal history approach claim that "neither the concepts of the humanities, nor those of the social sciences or of the natural sciences can enable us to understand adequately the crisis of the relationship of nature to society" (Kluge & Schramm 1989: 63), because nature and society have become an indissoluble unity in the industrial process. A proposed solution to the apparent conflict is that the fiction of an essential distinction between nature and society be abandoned (ibid.).

Sieferle's universal history approach postulates precisely this unity of culture and nature. The only explanation for this view is that the above-mentioned shift in perspective has indeed taken place: the unity of culture and nature occurs within culturally constituted history and not within nature or within the history of nature, that is evolution. Our suspicions are confirmed in Kluge & Schramm (1989: 63), who state that the distinction between nature and society is to be resolved "as a historical one", and that technology and science are to be understood as a social project and "cultural modernization".

The unity of nature and culture within culture: the cultural ecology approach

One possibility of conceiving the unity of nature and culture within culture is the cultural ecology approach. Cultural ecology explicitly investigates the relationship between culture and nature (Bargatzky 1986: 13) – more precisely stated, the relationship between social systems and their natural environments (Bargatzky 1986: 92). Such relationships include simple feedback processes, but they are not limited to them (as in Bennett). In contrast to ecology, which, as a natural science, deals with the relationship of organisms to their animate and inanimate environments, cultural ecology includes humankind and investigates the particular structure of the relationship between humans and nature as a consequence of cultural achievements. Accordingly, nature is the subject of cultural ecology – not intact nature, untouched by human beings, but nature as it is formed and changed by them. This we shall call "cultured" nature.

Cultural ecology understood in these terms connects culture and nature in terms of the social organization of humankind. This is far more encompassing, in the sense of differentiated cultural autonomy, than Steward's mere environmental adaptation of culture. "Subjective components" such as intentions, motives, feelings, understanding and values are at least just as important as "objective components" such as rocks, water, animals, plants, metabolism and entropy. The programme of cultural ecology, then, is designed to explain the relationships between these two components (Bargatzky 1986: 19). A more comprehensive formulation of this can be found in Meyer-Abich (1988: 103), who states that the subject of the cultural sciences is humankind in its relationship to nature. This also includes nature itself. From this follows the necessity, therefore, to perceive the relationship of humankind to nature as a part of cultural reality, and to make it the subject of cultural study. An explicit precondition here is that man be understood as a social and natural being (ibid.).

From the perspective of cultural ecology, nothing precludes the idea of defining meaningful work in cultural studies as the investigation of the relationship between humankind and nature. The question that does arise, however, is whether such an approach (generally presented as a holistic claim) should constitute the entire programme of cultural studies. It is conceivable

149

that cultural studies researchers would find other subjects at least as important as the specific issue of the culturally determined relationship between humankind and nature. What, then, is the subject of cultural studies?

Heinrich Rickert, following Hermann Paul, propagated the idea of cultural studies (*Kulturwissenschaft*) as an alternative to the humanities (*Geisteswissenschaft*). According to Rickert (1926: 18–22), culture is suffused with value. Cultural objects are things imbued with value, in contrast to nature, which is the embodiment of those things that emerge on their own – perceptible, incomprehensible being, devoid of meaning. Culture is meaningful and comprehensible; religion, the Church, law, the state, customs and mores, science, language, literature, art, the economy and the technical means necessary for its functioning are all cultural objects (ibid.; Rickert also explicitly includes here such things as agricultural equipment, including machines and chemicals).

Finally, Rickert defines culture as "the totality of existing objects bound to generally recognized values – or to meaningful structures defined by such values – cultivated with due consideration for these values" (ibid.: 28).[1] The terms he emphasizes here are "values" and "cultivation". This concept of culture is quite comprehensive. Correspondingly, the term "cultural studies" thus designates all the disciplines other than those subsumed under the natural sciences and mathematical sciences (today, we would speak of the combined social sciences and liberal arts or humanities (ibid.: 22). On the basis of Rickert's arguments, therefore, we may conclude that although cultural ecology is only a subdiscipline, its claim is very far-reaching because it has at its core the unity of nature and culture within culture.

Culture, nature and theory of action

Action between culture and nature occurs on several levels. In accordance with philosophical tradition one can distinguish the following levels and types set out in Table 8.1:

The purpose of these two lists is less to present an exhaustive overview than to show the broad spectrum of cultural action. Science, for instance, is ascribed to the cultural level of action, "theory", which produces the action type, "knowledge". Although conventional interpretations of science, as well as the linguistic origin of *theoria*, suggest a passive, contemplative–receptive orientation, modern theories of knowledge have repeatedly emphasized the active subject, who must virtually conquer the object of knowledge.

Further, technology based on mathematics is preformed by the physical

---

1. ". . . die Gesamtheit der realen Objekte, an denen allgemein anerkannte Werte oder durch sie konstituierte Sinngebilde haften, und die mit Rücksicht auf diese Werte gepflegt werden."

Table 8.1 Levels and types of action.

Level of action	Type of action
Theory	Knowledge
Aesthetics	Perception
Ethics	Justification of norms
Politics	Implementation of norms
Planning	Regulation
Economy and technology	Production

sciences, and both are compatible with the theory and practice of economic activity in terms of exploitation of nature for the satisfaction of human needs. What we produce, we grasp cognitively and what we grasp cognitively, we can also produce and suffuse with value (cf. §1.2). Picht (1989: 10), for example, stresses the point that modern science and technology, including industrial production, are to be seen as a unit. The structural identity of cognition, action, valuation and norm setting is made clear once it is viewed from the perspective of cultural action.

Cultural instruments regulate action between culture and nature. Such regulation is called planning – that is future-orientated action aimed at implementation. The cultural instruments of planning are taken from science, technology, economics and law. Although doubts may be raised as to whether the interaction between human beings and nature can be planned (i.e. as to the feasibility or credibility of planning), this does not change the fact that plans continue to be made. In this sense human ecology is concerned with actions, which are understood in the widest sense to include knowledge, implementation, evaluation and planning, although the goals may be different. The following proposition could also be a premise in human ecology: planning measures that result in the destruction of the biosphere may also lead to a decline in global culture. But what is global culture, and what is the meaning of its decline in connection with crises in nature?

8.4 The crisis of nature as a cultural crisis – prerequisites for controlling instability

The common foundation of global culture is the industrial utilization of nature by means of science and technology. Global culture is global industrial culture and this can lead to the end of cultural evolution if it undermines its own possibilities for variation, thus eradicating cultural change. The "gene banks" for cultural development contain regional identities as well as the identities of social groups and minorities. All of these ensure tolerance in the spectrum of cultural variation. If this variation is lost, then the potential for change and development will also decline. We can already observe a general trend towards accommodation and pressure to eliminate distinctions through uniformity of consumer values and the development towards a uniform, worldwide economic order (determined, in part, by the international debt crisis).

In agriculture, a decline in ecological and cultural diversity can already be observed. One reason for this may be that nature–culture interaction in agriculture is direct – its consequences are immediate. Global agriculture, as an economic hypersystem, has reduced the original multiplicity of cultivated plants to a handful of gradually languishing species; it has been forced to set up seed banks to reconstruct artificially the natural diversity that has been lost.

Apart from this, people have begun thinking about ways to preserve not only genetic diversity, but cultural diversity as well, in the productive use of land – for instance, promoting regional agrarian cultures instead of the global food production monoculture, encouraging pursuit of "the breadwinning arts" instead of production of food solely for economic survival and export. Such will be the alternative (Glaeser 1986, Groeneveld 1987).

Analogous to the decline in human (agrarian) culture, is there danger of a self-induced decline in nature? We usually speak of natural crisis when the equilibrium of ecological systems has been irreversibly destabilized – that is, when exogenic influences are so great that nature's self-regulative processes are unable to restore the regulative balance *and* the natural system shifts to a less diversified state. Since even given ecological equilibrium processes are irreversible, they are, in terms of the physics of evolution, in a state of (thermodynamic) non-equilibrium: they export entropy, that is, they gain information. The concept of natural crisis, therefore, cannot be easily integrated into the terminology of evolutionary physics. It can by no means be identified with non-equilibrium.

Is the linking of the two concepts, natural crisis and imbalance, evidence for an anthropocentric fallacy? It is usually not natural ecosystems that are being observed, but human ecological systems, that is, systems in which humankind plays a culturally structuring or formative role. For us, the disruption of an equilibrium in nature expresses itself socially. The social system becomes an indicator for natural equilibrium. So-called natural crises are therefore actually social crises and can be recognized as such. We would not speak of "crisis" in reference to the birth or death of a galaxy, or in reference to the creation or annihilation of biosystems remote from humankind. Instead, we apply the terms "evolution", "transformation" or "change".

Even the so-called Big Bang, more recently interpreted as the heat death, occurring 15 000 million years ago and marking the beginning of time (irreversibility), matter and life, and ultimately interpreted as the origin of nature (Prigogine 1989: 56–9), can hardly be called a natural crisis.

The heat death lies behind, not ahead of us. The universe began . . . with a gigantic, entropic explosion – an enormous, irreversible process that, at the same time, set the arrow of time in flight. Time and the universe were born in the same manner. (Prigogine 1989: 56)

The evolutionary sequence is as follows. First there was space–time, then the vacuum that gave rise to black holes; these, in turn, created matter and the universe with which we are familiar (Prigogine 1989: 58 f.). All of these are irreversible processes. This means that the universe has arisen out of instability.

In contrast, the oil crisis, the agricultural crisis, and the manifold crises arising from the industrial exploitation of nature (such as the hole in the ozone layer and global warming) are not only anthropocentric, but also anthropogenic crises. By means of the instruments they have created during their cultural evolution, human beings have altered local natural equilibria in order to obtain certain social benefits. Following its own laws, nature strives to achieve a new stability by means of readjustment, which humankind experiences as deadly catastrophes – floods, droughts, landslides and climatic changes, among others.

Why, then, do we speak of "crisis"? What is our purpose in using the word? The Greek word *krisis*, coming from *krinein* (to separate, divide), denotes a decisive situation, a turning point. In medicine, it refers to that stage of a feverish infection during which the future course of the illness is determined, that is, the development the history of the illness will take. This understanding of "crisis" can be transferred to other areas. On the one hand, it refers to the ability to experience – implying subjectivity – and, on the other, it refers to identity. In general, therefore, "crisis" refers to those significant stages of a process that enable subjects to recognize those turning points decisive for the development of a history whose course is identical with itself.

So much for the generalization. But can the "crisis of nature" be mapped onto this definition? It must be noted that the expression "history of nature" is used metaphorically, since, whereas nature in the course of its development is identical with itself, it is *not* a cognizing subject. Therefore, we cannot speak correctly either of a (subject-centred) natural crisis, in the strictest sense of the word, nor of nature that is "ailing". "Nature in crisis", then, is also nothing but a metaphor – an example of imprecise thinking. As such, this expression is indicative of a cultural misunderstanding.

If anything is in crisis it is culture, whereas the human society that has jeopardized the natural foundations of its own survival is ailing. That the human species should survive is as legitimate an interest as the survival of any other species, but this interest should not be confused with the interests of nature. On the other hand, the allusion to unclear thinking implies no claim as to what the relationship between culture and nature *should* be.

Social norms stipulating how humankind should deal with nature cannot be derived from nature. This fact has no influence whatsoever, positively or negatively, on the truth of such norms. Human society, in contrast to nature, selects its own goals. The norms guiding society's behaviour towards nature require us to seek and to establish the cultural and natural conditions under which the species *Homo sapiens*, as a cultural parasite within the metabolism of nature, can survive: How can humankind, with the aid of cultural instruments, interact with nature such that a steady approach towards the goal of sustainable use of natural resources can be achieved?

This is a genuine question, perhaps the central one, of human ecology. As with philosophical questions, many different natural sciences and cultural disciplines are challenged to answer it. But it is not clear which of the natural science disciplines or the humanities might be able to satisfy this demand, because, "not even in the natural sciences ... is nature spoken of; and because of that, they have access to no knowledge that would be able to arrest the destruction of nature" (Picht 1989: 11). Moreover, as Picht emphasizes, "a science that destroys nature cannot provide true knowledge of nature" (Picht 1989: 11).

Thus, anthropocentric self-interest requires from us not only knowledge, but also the ethical and political will to redetermine the active interrelationship between culture and nature. But cultural evolution has so far largely neglected the instruments of (ecological) politics and ethics.

8.5 Conclusion

This may be considered the message of this volume, which may appear to be a heterogeneous collection of theoretical considerations, ethical–political postulates and demands, and empirical examples and applications. The unifying factors are human ecology and the nature–culture relationship; at the same time the book comprises both an analytical and a normative approach. Although, analytically, we are compelled to spell out a clear distinction between nature, culture and the notion of crisis, including the fact that nature in no way prescribes us what to do and how to do it, normatively, human ethics, politics and policies – that is the interests of humankind as a whole or of particular societies – guide our behaviour and actions, including those that directly or indirectly affect nature.

In reality, abuse of the natural human environment often occurs due to short-sighted interests that are not in line with global sustainable survival. Significantly, global environmental degradation is often referred to as "global environmental change", an obvious ideological euphemism that serves interest-bound, normative purposes. Although this euphemism seems to reflect the analytical arguments against "nature in crisis" or "ailing nature" presented above, in truth, the line of reasoning is purposely confused; such terminology, professing an adherence to natural laws, actually disguises short-term, exploitative vested interests.

If nature's interests appear not to differentiate between *Homo sapiens* and other animal species, in particular as regards their survival, there seems to be a simple biological answer. If humankind wishes to achieve sustainable use of natural resources and of natural absorption capacities, as other animals do, then the natural controls that maintain the ecosystem for other species but are hardly applicable and certainly not acceptable to humans, must be replaced by human, cultural controls. The problem for the human being is – and this is why the biological answer is too simple – actually achieving self-organized cultural control that would have to comprise two things: the insight that sustainable behaviour is necessary, and the political will to implement measures that reflect that insight. This complex issue calls for a policy that integrates several domains, namely, environment, development and agriculture, and it has to be feasible for both the northern and southern political spheres.

Of course, the success of such a venture requires long-term planning and cannot be achieved with any great speed. The object of this book was to point out some of the conditions for success or failure from a variety of perspectives, approaching the question holistically in the tradition of human ecology.

References

Adekayi, P., A. A. Adepetu, E. Aguigwo, A. D. Kidd, U. J. Meekyaa, C. Oche, K. Ologe, K. D. Phillips-Howard, F. A. Sunmaila 1990. *Prioritization of problems in the Jos Plateau tin mining region: a research formulation exercise*. Jos Plateau Environmental Resources Development Programme (JPERDP) Interim Report 16, Department of Geography, University of Durham.

Ahmed, F. 1987. Siege of Balasore. *India Today* (15 March), 62–3.

Aird, J. S. 1990. *Slaughter of the innocents: coercive birth control in China*. Washington DC: AEI Press.

Anon. 1979. *The environmental protection law of the People's Republic of China (for trial implementation)*. Beijing: Renmin (People's Publisher).

— 1994. *China's Agenda 21. White Paper on China's population, environment and development in the 21st century*. Beijing: China Environmental Science Press.

Aristotle 1961. *Metaphysics*. London/Cambridge, Mass.: Heinemann/Harvard University Press.

Ayres, R. U. & A. V. Kneese 1969. Production, consumption and externalities. *American Economic Review* **59**, 282–97.

Bargatzky, T. 1986. *Einführung in die Kulturökologie. Umwelt, Kultur und Gesellschaft*. Berlin: Reimer.

Barrows, H. H. 1923. Geography as human ecology. *Association of American Geographers, Annals* **13**, 1–4.

Bätzing, W. 1985. *Die Alpen. Naturbearbeitung und Umweltzerstörung*, 3rd edn. Frankfurt: Sendler.

— 1988. Umweltkrise und reproduktive Arbeit. *Kommune* **5**, 69–79.

Bennett, J. W. 1976. *The ecological transition: cultural anthropology and human adaptation*. New York: Pergamon.

Bennett, R. J. & R. J. Chorley 1978. *Environmental systems: philosophy, analysis and control*. London: Methuen.

Betke, D. 1983. Forstpolitik: Schutz und Entwicklung des Waldes. See Glaeser (1983a), 251–99.

— 1989. Die Umweltfrage. See Louven (1989), 54–82.

Bews, J. W. 1935. *Human ecology*. London: Oxford University Press.

Binswanger, H. C. 1989. Ökologisch orientierte Wirtschaftswissenschaft. See Glaeser (1989a), 143–52.

Bodenstedt, A. 1986. Die Entwicklung agrarkultureller Wesenszüge in Europa. See Glaeser (1986), 49–63.

— 1990. Rural culture – a new concept. *Sociologia Ruralis* **30**(1), 34–47.

Borden, R. J. 1989. From ecology to human ecology – and back again: a commentary on Young's contribution to an integrated human ecology. *Acta Oecologiae Hominis* **1**, 137–43.

Borgstrom, G. 1973. The breach in the flow of mineral nutrients. *Ambio* **2**, 129–35.

Bornkamm, R. 1971. Grundprinzipien der Ökologie. *Der mathematische und naturwissenschaftliche Unterricht* **24**, 467–72.

Boyden, S. 1979. *An integrative ecological approach to the study of human settlements* [MAB Technical Notes 12]. Paris: UNESCO.

BMU (ed.) 1991. *Ökologischer Aufbau. Eckwerte der ökologischen Sanierung und Entwicklung in den neuen Ländern*. Bonn: Bundesministerium für Umwelt, Naturschutz und Reaktorsicherheit.

Bruckmeier, K. & P. Teherani-Krönner 1992. Agrarian cultures: the application of a human-ecological paradigm into the sociological analysis of rural society. Paper presented at the Eighth World Congress for Rural Sociology, 11–16 August 1992, Pennsylvania State University.

Bruckmeier, K., B. Glaeser and H. Grund 1995. *Implementation of three EU water directives. European Union project: Conditions for the integration of European Community environmental policy at the local level. German National Report and Case Study* [mimeograph]. Berlin: Science Center Berlin (WZB).

Bruhn, J. G. 1974. Human ecology: a unifying science? *Human Ecology* **2**, 105–25.

Buntzel, R. 1986. Eindrücke von einer Agrarkultur in der industriellen Wachstumsgesellschaft: Eine Fallstudie aus Hohenlohe/Württemberg. See Glaeser (1986), 31–46.

Callicott, J. B. & R. T. Ames (eds) 1989. *Nature in Asian traditions of thought: essays in environmental philosophy*. Albany: State University of New York Press.

Cannon, T. & A. Jenkins 1990. *The geography of contemporary China: the impact of Deng Xiaoping's decade*. London: Routledge.

Chambers, R. 1988. *Sustainable livelihoods, environment and development: putting poor rural people first*. Discussion Paper 240, Institute of Development Studies, University of Sussex.

Chan, K. W. & X. Xu 1985. Urban population growth and urbanization in China since 1949: reconstructing baseline. *The China Quarterly* **104**, 583–613.

Cheng, X, C. Han & D. C. Taylor 1992. Sustainable agricultural development in China. *World Development* **20**(8), 1127–44.

Chin, Y-L. 1980. Chinese philosophy. *Social Sciences in China* **1**, 83–93.

Clapham Jr, W. B. 1980. Environmental problems, development and agricultural production systems. *Environmental Conservation* **7**, 145–52.

— & R. F. Pestel 1978. *A common framework for integrating the economic and ecologic dimensions of human ecosystems ii: processes and problem chains within the natural stratum*. Research Memorandum RM–78–30, IIASA, Laxenburg (Austria).

Conrad, J. 1990. *Nitrate pollution and politics: Great Britain, the Federal Republic of Germany and the Netherlands*. Aldershot, England: Avebury/Gower.

Conway, G. R. 1987. The properties of agro-ecosystems. *Agricultural Systems* **24**, 95–117.

Craik, H. 1970. Environmental psychology. *New Directions in Psychology* **4**, 3–101.

Daele, W. van den 1992. The research program of the section "norm-building and environment". Discussion paper FS II 92–301, Science Center Berlin (WZB.)

Delft Hydraulics Laboratory 1981. *Analysing biospheric changes*. Working Document E1537-D001, prepared for the IFIAS, Delft.

Dice, L. R. 1955. *Man's nature and nature's Man: the ecology of human communities*. Ann Arbor: University of Michigan Press.

Diemer, A. & I. Frenzel (eds) 1958. *Philosophie [Das Fischer Lexikon]*. Frankfurt, M.: Fischer.

Drieschner, M. 1981. *Einführung in die Naturphilosophie*. Darmstadt: Wissenschaftliche Buchgesellschaft.

Dunlap, R. E. 1980. Paradigmatic change in social science: from human exemptions to an ecological paradigm. *American Behavioral Scientist* **24**, 5–14.

Dürr, H-P. 1989. Wissenschaft und Wirklichkeit. Über die Beziehung zwischen dem Weltbild der Physik und der eigentlichen Wirklichkeit. In *Geist und Natur. Über den Widerspruch naturwissenschaftlicher Erkenntnis und philosophischer Welterfahrung*, H-P. Dürr & W. Ch. Zimmerli (eds), 28–46. Bern: Scherz.

Eder, K. 1988. *Die Vergesellschaftung der Natur. Studien zur sozialen Evolution der praktischen Vernunft*. Frankfurt, M.: Suhrkamp.

Egger, K. 1979. Ökologie als Produktivkraft: Erfahrungen bei "eco-farming" in Ostafrika. In *Agrarreform in der Dritten Welt*, H. Elsenhans (ed.), 217–54. Frankfurt: Campus.

Egger, K. & B. Martens 1987. Theory and methods of ecofarming and their realization in Rwanda, East Africa. See Glaeser (1987b), 150–75.

Ellen, R. 1982. *Environment, subsistence and system: the ecology of small-scale social formations*. Cambridge: Cambridge University Press.

Enzensberger, H. M. 1973. Zur Kritik der politischen Ökologie. In *Ökologie und Politik oder die Zukunft der Industrialisierung* [Kursbuch 33], H. M. Enzensberger & K. M. Michel (eds), 1–42. Berlin: Rotbuch.

Eyre, S. R. & G. R. J. Jones 1966. *Geography as human ecology: methodology by example*. London: Edward Arnold.

Fietkau, H-J. 1989. Vom Umgang mit ökologischer Komplexität aus Sicht der humanistischen Psychologie. See Glaeser (1989a), 119–27.

Fischer, M. 1989. Luftreinhaltung zwischen industrieller Revolution und humanökologischem Gleichgewicht. See Glaeser (1989a), 225–52.

Forrester, J. W. 1971a. *World dynamics*. Cambridge, Mass.: Wright-Allen.

— 1971b. Counter-intuitive behavior of social systems. *Technology Review* **73**(3), 1–16. (Reprinted 1975 in *Collected papers of Jay W. Forrester*, 211–44. Cambridge, Mass.: Wright-Allen Press.)

— 1971c. *Churches at the transition between growth and world equilibrium*. Cambridge, Mass.: Institute of Technology (mimeographed paper). (Reprinted 1975 in *Collected papers of Jay W.Forrester*, 255–69. Cambridge, Mass.: Wright-Allen Press.)

Franke, M. 1986. Maniok zwischen Agrarkultur und Weltwirtschaft. See Glaeser (1986), 151–62.

Friday, L. & R. Laskey (eds) 1991. *The fragile environment: new approaches to global problems*. Cambridge: Cambridge University Press.

Friedland, E. I. 1977. Values and environmental modeling. See Hall & Day (1977), 115-31.

Friend, G. 1978. Closing the cycle. *Mazingira* **7**, 47–52.

Friend, J. & A. Hickling 1987. *Planning under pressure: the strategic choice approach*. Oxford: Pergamon.

Frissel, M. J. (ed.) 1977. Cycling of mineral nutrients in agricultural ecosystems. *Agro-ecosystems* **4**, 1–354.

Fürst, D. 1989. Ökologisch orientierte Raumplanung. See Glaeser (1989a), 170–80.

Glaeser, B. 1980. Humanökologie: Das sozialwissenschaftliche Paradigma. In *Proceedings of the Second Vienna International Meeting on Human Ecology (May 16–21, 1977)*, H. Knötig (ed.), 69–73. Vienna: Archivum Oecologiae Hominis.

— (ed.) 1982. *Ökologie und Umweltschutz in der VR China*. Bochum: Brockmeyer.

— (ed.) 1983a. *Umweltpolitik in China. Modernisierung und Umwelt in Industrie, Landwirtschaft und Energieerzeugung*. Bochum: Brockmeyer.

— 1983b. Entwicklungspolitik und Umweltproblematik in China. See Glaeser (1983a), 9–44.

— (ed.) 1984. *Ecodevelopment: concepts, projects, strategies*. Oxford: Pergamon Press.

— (ed.) 1986. *Die Krise der Landwirtschaft. Zur Renaissance von Agrarkulturen*. Frankfurt . M.: Campus.

— (ed.) 1987a. *Learning from China? Development and environment in Third World countries*. London: Allen & Unwin.

— 1987b. *The Green Revolution revisited*. London: Allen & Unwin.

— 1988. *Environmental policy. The example of the Federal Republic of Germany in the international context*. Bonn: Friedrich-Ebert-Stiftung.

— (ed.) 1989a. *Humanökologie. Grundlagen präventiver Umweltpolitik*. Opladen, Germany: Westdeutscher.

— 1989b. An eco-development approach for the Andaman & Nicobar Islands. In *Economic development alternatives. Andaman & Nicobar Islands*, B. R. Virmani & K. J. Voll (eds), 120–31. New Delhi: Vision Books.

— 1990. The environmental impact of economic development: problems and policies. See Cannon & Jenkins (1990), 249–65.

— 1991. Umweltfolgen wirtschaftlicher Entwicklung in der VR China: Probleme und Politik. *Zeitschrift für Umweltpolitik und Umweltrecht* **14**(2), 197–208.

— 1995. *Housing for the poor: sustainable development in rural India*. Delhi/ London: Sage.

Glaeser, B. & P. Teherani-Krönner (eds) 1992. *Humanökologie und Kulturökologie*. Opladen, Germany: Westdeutscher.

Graumann, C. F. 1972. *Interaktion und Kommunikation* [Handbuch der Psychologie 7: Sozialpsychologie]. Göttingen: Hogrefe.

Groeneveld, S. 1986. Agrarkulturen statt Landwirtschaft: Entwurf einer Perspektive. See Glaeser (1986), 165–86.

— 1987. *Brotkünste. Texte zu Agrarberatung und Agrarkulturen*. Kassel: Gesamthochschul-Bibliothek.

Gustafsson, L. 1989. *Das seltsame Tier aus dem Norden*. München: Hanser (from the Swedish: *Det sällsamma djuret från norr*, Stockholm: Norstedts Förlag, 1989).

Habermas, J. 1967. *Theorie und Praxis*, 2nd edn. Neuwied: Luchterhand.

— 1985. *Die neue Unübersichtlichkeit*. Frankfurt, M.: Suhrkamp.

Haeckel, E. 1866. *Generelle Morphologie der Organismen. Band 2: Allgemeine Entwicklungsgeschichte der Organismen*. Berlin: Reimer.

— 1870. Über Entwicklungsgang und Aufgabe der Zoologie. Rede, gehalten beim Eintritt in die philosophische Facultät zu Jena am 12. Januar 1869. *Jenaische Zeitschrift für Medizin und Naturwissenschaft* **5**, 353–70.

Hagemann, E. & R. Pestel 1987. Agriculture as a component of China's modernization strategy. See Glaeser (1987a), 162–72.

Hall, C. A. S. & J. W. Day Jr (eds) 1977. *Ecosystem modeling in theory and practice*. New York: John Wiley.

Hartkopf, G. & E. Bohne 1983. *Umweltpolitik. Band 1: Grundlagen, Analysen und Perspektiven*. Opladen, Germany: Westdeutscher.

Hawley, A. H. 1944. Ecology and human ecology. *Social Forces* **22**, 398–405.

— 1950. *Human ecology: a theory of community structure*. New York: Ronald.

Hellpach, W. 1950 [1911]. *Geopsyche*, 6th edn. Stuttgart (Leipzig): Ehmke (Engelmann).

Hill, R. D. 1994. Upland development policy in the People's Republic of China. *Land Use Policy* **11**(1), 8–16.

Hoffmeister, J. (ed.) 1955. *Wörterbuch der philosophischen Begriffe*, 2nd edn. Hamburg: Felix Meiner.

Hu, A. & Y. Wang 1991. Current status, causes and remedial strategies of China's ecology and environment. *Chinese Geographical Science* **1**(2), 97–108.

Hu, A. & P. Zou 1991. *China's population development*. Beijing: China Science & Technology Press.

Huber, J. 1989. Eine sozialwissenschaftliche Interpretation der Humanökologie. See Glaeser (1989a), 57–75.

Imfeld, A. 1986a. Vom Überfluß zur Dürre im Sahel: Zerfall von Ackerbau und Pastoralismus. See Glaeser (1986), 85–102.

— 1986b. Die Entkolonialisierung des Mais in Afrika. See Glaeser (1986), 141–50.

Inglehart, R. 1990. *Culture shift in advanced industrial society*. Princeton, NJ: Princeton University Press.

IOHE (ed.) 1981. *Human ecology* [brochure]. Vienna: International Organization for Human Ecology.

Jänicke, M. & H. Weidner (eds) 1995. *Successful environmental policy. A critical evaluation of 24 cases*. Berlin: Edition Sigma.

Jansson, B.-O. 1980. The Baltic systems of man and nature. *Ambio* **9**, 112–13.

Jowett, J. 1990. People: demographic patterns and policies. See Cannon & Jenkins (1990), 102–32.

Kant, I. 1781. *Kritik der reinen Vernunft*, 1st edn. Riga: Hartknoch.

— 1785. *Grundlegung zur Metaphysik der Sitten*. Riga: Hartknoch. (*Groundwork of the metaphysic of morals*, translated by H. J. Paton. London: Routledge, 1993.)

— 1787. *Kritik der reinen Vernunft*, 2nd edn. Riga: Hartknoch. (*Critique of pure reason*, V. Politis (ed.). London: Dent, 1991.)

— 1788. *Kritik der praktischen Vernunft*. Riga: Hartknoch. (*Critique of practical reason*, translated by L. W. Beck. New York: Macmillan, 1993.)

— 1799. *Kritik der Urteilskraft*, 3rd edn (1st edn 1790). Berlin: Lagarde. (*Critique of judgment*, translated by W. S. Pluhar. Indianapolis: Hackett, 1987.)

Kim, H-S. & H. Michel-Kim 1986. Die koreanische Agrarkultur zwischen Tradi-

161

tion und Zukunft. See Glaeser (1986), 111–28.

King, F. H. 1911. *Farmers of forty centuries of permanent agriculture in China, Korea and Japan*. Madison, Wisconsin: Mrs F. H. King (4th impression 1949, edited by B. J. Cape).

Kinzelbach, W. K. H. 1987. Energy and environment in China. See Glaeser (1987a), 173–84.

Kirsch, G. 1989. Prävention und menschliches Handeln. See Glaeser (1989a), 255–65.

Klaus, G. & M. Buhr (eds) 1976. *Philosophisches Wörterbuch*, 12th edn. Leipzig: Enzyklopädie.

Kluge, T. & E. Schramm 1989. Geschichte als Naturschauspiel? *Freibeuter* **40**, 56–65.

Kölsch, O. 1989. Humanökologische Forschung für Landwirtschaft und Agrarpolitik. See Glaeser (1989a), 181–93.

Koslowski, P. 1985. Die Grenzen der ökonomischen Theorie. *Merkur* **39**(9/10), 791–806.

Koth, M. 1987. Schutz von Umwelt und Natur. *Der Tagesspiegel* (6 March), 19.

Leach, G. 1976. *Energy and food production*. Guildford, England: IPC Science and Technology Press.

Leipert, C. 1989. Integrierte Beschäftigungs- und Umweltpolitik. See Glaeser (1989a), 153–69.

Leitzmann, C., W. Sichert, U. Hixt 1986. Entstehung von Agribusiness und Untergang der Agrarkultur am Beispiel Zuckerrohr. See Glaeser (1986), 131–9.

Levine, N. (ed.) 1975. *Human ecology*. Belmont, California: Duxbury.

Lockeretz, W., R. Klepper, B. Commoner, M. Gertler, M. Fast, D. O'Leary, R. Blobaum 1975. A comparison of the production, economic patterns and energy intensiveness of corn belt farms that do and do not use inorganic fertilizers and pesticides. CBNS-Ae 4, St Louis, Missouri: Washington University.

Louven, E. (ed.) 1989. *China zu Beginn der 90er Jahre: Strukturen und Reformen – ein Handbuch*. Hamburg: Institut für Asienkunde.

Lünzer, I. 1992. Rohstoff- und Energiebilanzen aus ökologischer Sicht. In *Ökologische Landwirtschaft: Landbau mit Zukunft*, H. Vogtmann (ed.), 277–302. Karlsruhe: Müller.

Mao, Zedong 1965. *Selected works of Mao Tse-Tung*, vol. 1. Beijing: Renmin (People's Publisher).

Markl, H. 1986. *Natur als Kulturaufgabe*. Stuttgart: Deutsche Verlags-Anstalt.

McKenzie, R. D. 1925. The ecological approach to the study of the human community. In *The city*, R. E. Park, E. W. Burgess, R. D. McKenzie (eds), 63–79. Chicago: University of Chicago Press.

Meyer-Abich, K. M. 1984a. *Wege zum Frieden mit der Natur. Praktische Naturphilosophie für die Umweltpolitik*. München: Hanser.

— 1984b. Lauter schöne neue Abziehbilder. *Der Spiegel*, 7 May 1992.

— 1988. *Wissenschaft für die Zukunft. Holistisches Denken in ökologischer und gesellschaftlicher Verantwortung*. München: Beck.

Ministry of Agriculture, People's Republic of China 1992. China's policies and planning on sustainable agriculture and rural development – technical report to FAO. Office of National Agro-Regional Planning Committee, Ministry of Agriculture, People's Republic of China.

Moebius, K. 1877. *Die Auster und die Austernwirtschaft*. Berlin: Wiegandt, Hempel & Parey.

Needham, J. 1954–86. *Science and civilization in China*, vols 1–7. Cambridge: Cambridge University Press.

Newbould, J. 1973. The contribution of ecology to the study of human ecology. In *The education of human ecologists*, P. Rogers (ed.), 37–48. London: Charles Knight.

New China News Agency 1969 [21 October]. Quoted in L. Orleans & R. P. Stuttmeier 1970, "The Mao ethic and environmental quality", *Science* **170**, 1173–6.

Newcombe, K. 1975. Energy use in the Hong Kong food system. *Agro-ecosystems* **2**, 253–76.

— 1977. Nutrient flow in a major urban settlement: Hong Kong. *Human Ecology* **5**, 179–208.

Odum, H. T. 1971. *Environment, power and society*. New York: John Wiley.

— 1977. Energy, value and money. See Hall & Day (1977), 173–96.

O'Sullivan, P. E. 1979. The ecosystem-watershed concept in the environmental sciences: a review. *International Journal of Environmental Studies* **13**, 273–81.

Park, R. E. & E. W. Burgess 1921. *Introduction to the science of sociology*. Chicago: University of Chicago Press.

Phillips-Howard, K. D. 1985. A human ecological model for studying the impact of development projects upon the Niger Delta. In *The Mangrove ecosystem of the Niger delta: proceedings of a workshop (May 19-23, 1980)*, C. B. Powell & B. H. R. Wilcox (eds), Port Harcourt, Nigeria: University of Port Harcourt.

— 1982. *What happened to agriculture's contribution? An independent assessment of phosphorus inputs to Lough Neagh, Northern Ireland*. Discussion Paper IIES-dp 82–5. Berlin: Wissenschaftszentrum Berlin.

— 1985. The anthropic catchment-ecosystem concept: an Irish example. *Human Ecology* **13**, 209–40.

— 1989. *Synthesis of research findings and recommendations of Phase 1*. Jos Plateau Environmental Resources Development Programme (JPERDP) Interim Report 13, Department of Geography. Durham: University of Durham.

— & B. Glaeser 1983. Comparative investigation of conceptual models in human ecology. *Science and Public Policy* (February), 10–20.

Picht, G. 1989. *Der Begriff der Natur und seine Geschichte*. Stuttgart: Klett-Cotta.

Pimentel, D., L. E. Hurd, A. C. Belotti, M. J. Forster, I. N. Oka, O. D. Sholes, R. J. Whitman 1973. Food production and the energy crisis. *Science* **182**, 443–9.

Pongratz, H. 1990. Cultural tradition and social change in agriculture. *Sociologia Ruralis* **30**(1), 5–17.

Pontius, A. 1971. Die Subjekt–Objekt-Beziehung in Begriffen von Kant und Jung. *Kant-Studien* **62**, 121–5.

Popper, K. R. 1982 [1934]. *Logik der Forschung*, 7th edn. Tübingen: J. C. B. Mohr (Paul Siebeck).

Priebe, H. 1985. *Die subventionierte Unvernunft. Landwirtschaft und Naturhaushalt*. Berlin: Siedler.

Prigogine, I. 1989. Die Wiederentdeckung der Zeit. Naturwissenschaft in einer Welt begrenzter Vorhersagbarkeit. In *Geist und Natur. Über den Widerspruch naturwissenschaftlicher Erkenntnis und philosophischer Welterfahrung*, H-P. Dürr & W. Ch. Zimmerli (eds), 47–60. Bern: Scherz.

Proshansky, H. M., W. H. Ittelson, L. C. Rivlin 1970. *Environmental psychology: people and their physical settings*. New York: Holt, Rinehart & Winston.

Pryce, R. 1977. *Approaches to the study of man and environment*. Unit 2 of Section 1 in course "Fundamentals of human geography", 45-90. Milton Keynes: Open University Press.

Pufendorf, U. von 1986. Über ökonomische Determinanten und soziokulturelle Perspektiven einer Überwindung des Agrarprotektionismus. See Glaeser (1986), 65–70.

Qu, G. 1990. China's environmental policy and world environmental problems. *International Environmental Affairs* 2(2), 103–8.

— 1991. *Environmental management in China*. Beijing: United Nations Environment Programme and China Environment Science Press.

— 1994. Present environmental problems and some strategic tasks. *Peace* 35, 11-14.

Randers, J. & Donella Meadows 1971. *The carrying capacity of our global environment: a look at the ethical alternatives*. Cambridge, Mass.: MIT Press.

Redclift, M. 1987. *Sustainable development: exploring the contradictions*. London: Methuen.

Reichardt, R. 1976. Prolegomena zu einer humanökologischen Ethik. In *Proceedings of the International Meeting on Human Ecology (Vienna, September 15–19, 1975)*, H. Knötig (ed.), 529–43. St Saphorin, Switzerland: Georgi.

— & U. Schöndorfer 1977. Ethics. *Colloquium Internationale* 2(2/4), 131–2.

Reidl, H. & P. Weichhart 1980. Land use patterns as the result of human adaptation to the natural environment: a short report on some projects concerning medium-scale man–environment systems. *Man–Environment Systems* 10, 251–62.

RCEES (Research Center for Eco-Environmental Sciences) 1993. Chinese Academy of Sciences, Annual Report 1992. Beijing: Office of Scientific and Technological Affairs.

Rickert, H. 1926. *Kulturwissenschaft und Naturwissenschaft*, 7th edn. Tübingen: Mohr.

Ronnenberg, A. 1973. *Ökonomische Aspekte der biologisch-dynamischen Wirtschaftsweise – Konsequenzen für den Einzelbetrieb und für den Produktmarkt*. Darmstadt: Verlag Lebendige Erde.

Ross, L. 1988. *Environmental policy in China*. Bloomington/Indianopolis: Indiana University Press.

Rottach, P. (ed.) 1988. *Ökologischer Landbau in den Tropen. Ecofarming in Theorie und Praxis*, 3rd edn. Karlsruhe: C. F. Müller.

Sachs, I. 1977. Environment and styles of development. *Vierteljahresberichte* 70, 243–56 [special issue on ecodevelopment, edited by B. Glaeser].

— 1980. Culture, ecology and development: redefining planning approaches. In *Human behavior and environment* (vol. 4), I. Altman, A. Rapoport, J. F. Wohlwill (eds), 319–43. New York: Plenum.

Sargent, F. (ed.) 1974. *Human ecology*. Amsterdam: North Holland.

Schaffer, H. 1986. Natur- und Umweltschutz. In *Bericht über eine Studienreise in der Volksrepublik China*, Universität für Bodenkultur (ed.), 714–59. Vienna: Eigenverlag Dr Oskar Brendl.

Scharping, T. 1989. Bevölkerungspolitik. See Louven (1989), 29–53.

Schelling, F. W. J. 1967 [1797]. Ideen zu einer Philosophie der Natur als Einleitung in das Studium dieser Wissenschaft. In *F. W. J. von Schellings sämtliche Werke*, vol. 1 [1856], vol. 2 [1857] (Stuttgart/Augsburg: J. G. Cotta'scher Verlag). Darmstadt: Wissenschaftliche Buchgesellschaft (unrevised, unchanged reprographic reprint).

Schenkel, W. 1982. Abfallwirtschaft. See Glaeser (1982), 273–301.

Schischkoff, G. (ed.) 1957. *Philosophisches Wörterbuch*, 14th edn. Stuttgart: Kröner.

Schöndorfer, U. 1976. Grundfragen einer humanökologischen Ethik. In *Proceedings of the International Meeting on Human Ecology (Vienna, September 15–19, 1975)*, H. Knötig (ed.), 525–7. St. Saphorin, Switzerland: Georgi.

Schröter, C. & O. Kirchner 1902. *Die Vegetation des Bodensees, zweiter Teil.* Lindau: J. T. Stettner.

Schubert, H. J. 1989. Zum Zusammenhang von Ethik und Macht am Beispiel Eigenarbeit. See Glaeser (1989a), 128–40.

Sen, P. K. 1962. *Land and people of the Andamans.* Calcutta: The Post-Graduate Book Mart.

Sieferle, R. P. 1989. Die universalgeschichtliche Struktur des Umweltproblems. *Freibeuter* **40**, 41–55.

Singh, N. I. 1978. *The Andaman story.* New Delhi: Vikas.

Skolimowski, H. 1981. *Eco-philosophy.* Boston: Marion-Boyars.

Smil, V. 1984. *The bad earth: environmental degradation in China.* New York/London: M. E. Sharpe/Zed.

Spengler, O. 1959. *Der Untergang des Abendlandes (1924)*; cited from abridged 1959 edition. München: C. H. Beck.

Steinhart, J. S. & C. E. Steinhart 1974. Energy use in the US food system. *Science* **184**, 307–16.

Sternfeld, E. 1984. *Umweltpolitik und Industrialisierung in der Volksrepublik China (1949–1985).* Berlin: Ute Schiller.

Stöckler, M. 1989. Was kann man heute unter Naturphilosophie verstehen? *Philosophia naturalis* **26**(1), 1–18.

Stoll, K. 1969. Höchsterträge und Qualitätserzeugung bei Obst und Gemüse als Düngungsproblem. *Qualitas Plantarum et Materiae Vegetabiles* **18** (1–3), 206–24.

Suess, E. 1875. Quoted in G. E. Hutchinson, 1970. The biosphere. *Scientific American* **223**(3), 45.

Summerer, S. 1989a. Voraussetzungen einer Umweltethik. See Glaeser (1989a), 97–112.

— 1989b. Vorsorge contra Nachsorge – Ist Umweltqualität planbar? See Glaeser (1989a), 272–85.

Tang, W-S. & A. Jenkins 1990. Urbanisation: processes, policies and patterns. See Cannon & Jenkins (1990), 203–23.

Teherani-Krönner, P. 1989. Humanökologisch orientierte Entwicklungsprojekte. See Glaeser (1989a), 194–208.

Thompson, B. A. 1977. Environment and development in South America. *Vierteljahresberichte* **70**, 279–304 [special issue on ecodevelopment, edited by B. Glaeser].

Tretter, F. 1989. Humanökologische Medizin. See Glaeser (1989a), 209–24.

UNCHE (United Nations Conference on the Human Environment) 1973. Declaration on the Human Environment. In *The results from Stockholm. Beiträge zur Umweltgestaltung*, Part A10, 17–22. Berlin: Erich Schmidt.

Universität für Bodenkultur (ed.) 1986. *Bericht über eine Studienreise in die Volksrepublik China*. Vienna: Eigenverlag Dr Oskar Brendl.

Vico, G.B. 1924 [1744]. *Die neue Wissenschaft*. Berlin: De Gruyter.

Wagner, R. G. 1987. Agriculture and environmental protection in China. See Glaeser (1987a), 127–43.

Wang, D. 1959. The most important scientific and technical successes of environmental science the past 10 years of the new China. *Renmin Baojian* **10**, 899–903; quoted in *Umweltpolitik und Industrialisierung in der Volksrepublik China (1949–1985)*, Sternfeld (1984), 8–9. Berlin: Ute Schiller.

Wang, R., J. Zhao, X. Dai (eds) 1990. *Human ecology in China*. Annual report of the Department of Systems Ecology, RCEES, Academia Sinica, 1989. Beijing: China Science & Technology Press.

Wang, R., J. Zhao, Z. Ouyang (eds) 1991. *Human systems ecology*. Department of Systems Ecology, RCEES, Chinese Academy of Sciences, 1990. Beijing: China Science & Technology Press.

Wang, W. (ed.) 1992. *Survival and development – a study of China's long-term development*. Beijing/New York: Science Press.

Weichhart, P. 1979. Remarks on the term environment. *Geojournal* **3**, 623–31.

— 1989a. Die Rezeption des humanökologischen Paradigmas. See Glaeser (1989a), 46–56.

— 1989b. Werte und die Steuerung von Mensch–Umwelt-Systemen. See Glaeser (1989a), 76–93.

— 1989c. Ist Prävention möglich? Anmerkungen zu den Thesen von Guy Kirsch. See Glaeser (1989a), 266–71.

Weidner, H. 1991. Umweltpolitik – auf altem Weg zu einer internationalen Spitzenstellung. In *Die Bundesrepublik in den achtziger Jahren: Innenpolitik, politische Kultur, Außenpolitik*, W. Süß (ed.), 137–52.

— 1995 (in prep.). Developments and main characteristics of environmental policy in Germany. In *Federalism and the environment: environmental policy-making in Australia, Canada, Germany, and US*, K. Holland, F. Morton, B. Galligan (eds). Westport, Connecticut: Greenwood.

Weinzierl, H. 1984. *Tag der Umwelt – Tag der Trauer*. Press release, BUND (Bund für Umwelt und Naturschutz Deutschland).

Weizsäcker, C. F. von 1989. Geist und Natur. In *Geist und Natur. Über den Widerspruch naturwissenschaftlicher Erkenntnis und philosophischer Welterfahrung*, H-P. Dürr & W. Ch. Zimmerli (eds), 17–27. Bern: Scherz.

Wilen, J. E. 1973. A model of economic system – ecosystem interaction. *Environment and Planning* **5**, 409–20.

Wolanski, N. 1989. Man–culture–ecosystems and human ecology: comment on Young's "interdisciplinary human ecology". *Acta Oecologiae Hominis* **1**, 144–60.

World Bank (ed.) 1981. *China: socialist economic development* [Annex B, (Vol. 3): Population, health and nutrition]. Washington: World Bank (Report No. 3391-CHA).

WCED (World Commission on Environment and Development) 1987a. *Our common future*. Oxford: Oxford University Press.

— 1987b. *Food 2000: policies for sustainable agriculture*. London: Zed Books.

Worthington, E. B. 1973. What is human ecology? In *The education of human ecologists*, P. Rogers (ed.), 7–14. London: Charles Knight.

Young, G. L. 1974. Human ecology as an interdisciplinary concept: a critical enquiry. *Advances in Ecological Research* **8**, 1–105.

— 1989. A conceptual framework for an interdisciplinary human ecology. *Acta Oecologiae Hominis* **1**, 1–136.

Yu, C-L. 1975. Der Kampf gegen die Umweltverschmutzung. *Befreiung* **3**, 52–61.

— 1987a. Economic reform and its impact on the environment in China. See Glaeser (1987a), 120–26.

— 1987b. On the reactions of Chinese culture against the Western challenge: the other side of modernization. See Glaeser (1987a), 13–31.

Yu, K-J. 1991. Translate the philosophical ideal into reality: feng-shui as applied human ecology. Paper presented at the International Conference on Human Ecology, Göteborg, Sweden, 9–14, June.

Zucchetto, J. 1975. Energy–economic theory and mathematical models for combining the systems of man and nature, case study: the urban region of Miami, Florida. *Ecological Modelling* **1**, 241–68.

Index